150 POEMS FROM POLAND

150 Poems from Poland

ELIGIUSZ DYMOWSKI
ARTUR GRABOWSKI
WOJCIECH KASS
KRZYSZTOF KOEHLER
ANDRZEJ KOTAŃSKI
JAKUB PACZEŚNIAK
ADRIANA SZYMAŃSKA
TERESA TOMSIA
MICHAŁ ZABŁOCKI

Translated by
CHARLES S. KRASZEWSKI

AROUCA
PRESS

ISBN: 978-1-998492-60-2 (pbk)
ISBN: 978-1-998492-61-9 (hc)

The cover image is a detail from *Tryptyk o nocy II*
[Triptych about the Night, II] by Rafał Pacześniak
(b. 1973), private collection; used by permission.

CONTENTS

MAYBE AN EXPLANATION, BUT NOT AN INTRODUCTION FOR REASONS THAT WILL BE INTRODUCED AND EXPLAINED BELOW
Charles S. Kraszewski

150 Poems from Poland (which actually contains 178 poems, but more of that later) is a rather unique anthology. Usually, a translator or editor will select the poets whom he or she wishes to present to the target audience along with the poems composed by said poets which he or she — rightly or wrongly, with varying degrees of insight — believes to be most important or most representative of the poets' body of work. And then he or she (or someone else) will write an introduction telling the reader about the manner in which the poets approach the craft of poetry and how their understanding of the art is reflected in the poems they write.

Both of these approaches have something of hubris in them. Anthologies are good and bad — some, such as George Steiner's *Penguin Book of Modern Verse Translation*, are simply brilliant — but in every case, one person is imposing his viewpoint on others, telling them what to think. There is hardly an anthology of poetry in the world today that doesn't infuriate someone by what it leaves out or by 'completely misrepresenting this or that poet' by the poems selected for inclusion. Think of an intelligent person from another planet being introduced to Shakespeare via an anthology consisting of *The Turtle and The Dove, King John, Coriolanus,* and the songs excerpted from the comedies.

In contrast, no one chose the poems included in *150 Poems from Poland* but the poets themselves. And no one's going to tell you what they think of the poets' approach to the craft, what poetry means for them, except the poets themselves, who have written *artes poeticae* especially for this purpose. You can't get anything straighter from the horse's mouth than that.

The anthology came about in this way. I am a translator of Polish literature. Although I chiefly concentrate on the classics, I have also worked with contemporary writers. One day, it occurred to me that, over the years of my professional work, I have had dealings with some really very good poets, many of whom have become my friends. I thought: Wouldn't it be great to collect samples of all of their work and present them to the English reader, who may be unfamiliar with what is going on in Poland today, poetically speaking? And then, since many of them are being presented to the English readership for the first time, wouldn't it be splendid if they themselves chose their own calling cards?

And so the idea of what I first called *Ten Poets from Poland* was born. I began contacting poets of my acquaintance, tentatively, with the idea of the anthology, asking them to:

1) Choose ten poems of their own, from any periods of their creativity, that they would like to present to the English reader as introductions to their poetic personae;

2) Write a short *ars poetica*, or essay, describing their views on poetry. What poetry is, what is it for, how and why is it written, etc. That's as much direction as I gave them. The essay was to be as free-flowing as they wanted it to be; to speak of poetry in any way they wished to speak of it, as long as in it they expressed what they felt is important about poetry, the art in which they are intimately engaged. And finally:

3) To mention, or acknowledge, or refer to a particular 'master' (or 'masters')—a poet (or poets) who had a particular influence on them. What I was looking for was not a self-criticism by the poet, who would exemplify how this or that particular poet is present in his or her writing, but rather: What was your first important contact with poetry? What was the poem or poet that, upon reading, so thrilled you that you not only fell in love with poetry, but decided to try and become a poet yourself?

Ten Poets from Poland, ten poems each, in other words, *One Hundred Polish Poems*—a nice round figure, and everybody gets the same space, everything's nice and even ... Except that in life there really are no round numbers, nothing's nice and even. When you come to think of it, looking at nature, *nice* and *even* are antonyms. The beauty of the real world is found in cragginess, in uneven shapes, excess here and dearth there ... well, maybe 'dearth' is more pejorative sounding than I would would wish, but you get the idea.

At any rate, I contacted the poets whose work is contained in *150* (actually 178) *Poems from Poland*, with all of whom I had worked before (say, translating their work for this or that periodical, and/or catalogues published by the Book Institute of Poland), most of whom I know personally, and several of whom I am proud to call my friends. To my great delight, all of these men and women responded positively to my invitation and, over the space of the past seven months or so, sent me the poems that they had chosen for inclusion and the essays that they wrote especially for this anthology. Although I've expressed my gratitude to each of them personally, let me do it one more time, 'publicly', here. I'm grateful, friends, for your kind participation and labour and humbled and touched by your trust in me as your English medium.

Now, not everyone I contacted responded to the invitation. I'm rather glad to report that those poets of my acquaintance who didn't respond, or who declined participation, were such as I've worked with only fleetingly and are rather strangers to me, both professionally and socially. (Otherwise, rejection by friends would have smarted. Like dogs, translators are people too.)

The reader will notice that there are only two female poets amongst the authors included in *150 Poems from Poland*. This is not because I do not read female poets or do not prize them. One of my favourite poets is Marianne Moore; another is Tedi López Mills, whom I have translated into both English and Polish. If everything were 'nice and even', this anthology would be half and half, or at least contain a larger representation of the work of the fairer sex. (Please don't groan. I won't hide the fact that I consider women more attractive than men—in more ways than one.) However, as it was entirely up to the poets whether or not they participated in the anthology, and how they wished to be represented if they did choose to participate, this too was out of my hands. One female poet whom I approached declined to participate on the grounds that she has her own translator into English and (I suppose so as not to hurt the feelings of the translator in question) did not want to work with another. A second female poet whom I approached responded in the positive, then ignored me for a while, then responded positively again to second and third queries, but kept on ignoring the reminders for submissions, until I just gave up on her. And then a third female poet whom I approached didn't respond at all. So, potentially (my fingers slipped on the keyboard writing the last word; it originally came out 'poetentially'), potentially there might have been five female poets to the seven male poets included, which would have been nice. But alas.

Just think: twelve (poets) times fifteen (poems) each would have brought us a 'nice and even' *180 Poems from Poland*, with everybody occupying the same space . . . But that was not to be, and I think it's better this way, with all the cragginess and unevenness; with apologies to Frank Zappa and the Mothers of Invention, one size never fits all, and a real jumble is preferable, as I see it, to artificial uniformity, which gives one the mistaken sense of everything being down-boilable to some essential standard, and as we know, God has created each one of us as uniquely individual human beings, no two of us are alike, so why should we pretend that it's any different with individual creativity? Writer A needs only three sentences to get an idea across, whereas Writer B needs four elaborate paragraphs. And while we admire the terseness of Writer A's style, aren't we glad for all that expansive elegance of Writer B? It would be a disservice to have Writer A pad his or her statement to some artificial volume, while to make Writer B pare his or her statement down to three lines would be to completely destroy his or her narrative individuality. Laurence Sterne is not Ernest Hemingway. Or to put it another way, for the guitar aficionados out there: John Frusciante can say more in a single, simple run than Gary Rossington in a fifteen-minute jam. 'Dani California' would lose all its tightness if that crisp solo was elephantised, but by the same token, does anyone, seriously, want to 'pare down' the jam at the end of 'Freebird'? No. God no.

So, some of the poets had no problem with my ten-poem limit. They chose the ten poems that, in their opinion (and their opinion is the best opinion) most effectively present them to a new readership, and although there was some back and forth over the months with one or two poets about how the poems work in English, and in one case, one poem was substituted for another that 'didn't work' as well as the poet thought it would, these poets were satisfied with the way they appeared reflected in a ten-faceted gem. With others, it was more of a problem. 'What you're asking us to do', one of them, a friend, said to me over a beer, 'is to pick and choose between our children. You're asking us which kid we love the most. How can I do that?' Personally, I think that his metaphor is a bit drastic. And at any rate, considering my own (admittedly stunted and miserable) poetic progeny, I would have no problem with what Gerard Manley Hopkins once called the 'slaughter of the innocents'. But I appreciate my friend's devotion to his work, and the point is a good one.

One thing I refused to do was choose the poems myself. That went against the very premise of the anthology, and when — in more than one case — a poet sent me more than the required ten and said 'you choose which ones you want to use', I said, flatly, 'No'. This was to be a collection of self-portraits, and any interference of mine in the way a poet was represented would be to taint the batch. (Apologies for mixing metaphors. That's why I'm a translator, not a poet.) And so, when it turned out that there wasn't going to be the 'nice and even' participation of ten poets, but only nine at best, and that some of the poems included here are of haiku-like brevity, while others are short narratives that cover three or four pages, and that everything was going to be craggy and uneven anyway, I decided (curiously enough, over the objection of that same friend of mine who was hesitant to choose amongst his 'children') to include all the poems sent me by all the poets, except in the case of one of them, who'd sent a much bigger collection than the others, which needed to be pared down. By him. In other cases, I contacted those who'd sent only ten, informing them of the decision to broaden each section and giving them the opportunity of submitting more. Some did, some didn't.

With the essays, it was much the same thing. Some of the poets were hesitant to try and explain 'what poetry is' in prose, which is as much as to say 'poetry is what I give you—figure it out yourself'. I'm not being snarky or bitter here—this zen-like approach to poetics is commendable and valid. And yet, I made them do it (one of the participants here jokingly, but appropriately, refers to me 'calling him to the blackboard', and what student can refuse that, even if he does get up from his desk reluctantly?) so that the anthology would be even in that respect—here are my poems, here's what I think about poetry. Others (the more metaphysical of a very metaphysical bunch) reminded me that 'so many poets go into the making of a poet, how can I point out just one that set me on the road to where I am today?' Again, I have no problem with that. In my case, that poet is Thomas Hardy. Pure and simple. Yet I accept that other perspective as well. And so, on the one hand, we have some terse *artes poeticae*, which fit into my initially suggested scheme of 'four A4 pages of typescript', while in others, the description of what poetry is and the description of the road taken by the poet to arrive at his or her poetic identity are so detailed, that for clarity's sake, they had to be broken down into two essays. Once more, the world is either nice or even. Nice is real; I prefer real, as I'm sure you do as well, gentle Reader.

150 Poems from Poland, being an anthology created by the poets themselves and only translated by me, is about as objective a book as you can get. The reader might object (no pun intended) that it is rather subjective, because even if these poets chose their own poems and speak in their own voices about poetry, still and all, I chose the poets in the first place. And so how representative is this selection of what's going on in Polish poetry today, anyway?

It's a valid question, but I reckon out of place. First of all, I cast a wider net than my haul suggests. The book would be similar, but different, and certainly more varied, had those poets (female and male, at least in one case) who declined to participate actually tossed in their proverbial three cents.

Second, as far as the representative nature of the book is concerned, I couldn't do any better than I have done. My whole premise was to showcase the work of poets I have dealt with in the past and whose work I particularly admire. I don't know or work with every poet creative in Poland today. I'll get back to that statement in a moment. I couldn't send out a casting call to all Polish poets. To toy with impossibilities, if every one of them replied, the task would be too great for one person; we'd be talking about a series, if not a library, of Polish poetry, not a reasonably sized anthology. In a more probable scenario, given that my guiding principle was not to edit or exclude, I wouldn't be able to winnow down the contents myself; the picture that the reader would be getting of the landscape of contemporary Polish poetry would be incomplete anyway, skewed again by which poets actually chose to participate.

To get back to my admiration of the poets included here. Whether or not the reader is holding in his or her hands a wide representation of the state of contemporary Polish poetry, in these nine poets presented, he or she is holding a collection of very good poetry. Of course, being the translator, I don't want to be misunderstood as suggesting that these *translations* are very good. That's not for me to decide. What I can state, unequivocally, is that every single poem found in this anthology is very good in the original Polish. To the reader interested in Polish poetry, or poetry in general, I am confident that in the present book I am offering him or her a collection of the work of nine poets who are worth getting to know.

As I say, I am a professional translator. I work on commission, and despite tempting offers of remuneration, I sometimes turn down a commission when the original offered is a bad fit for me. I only translate works that I like, works to which, I feel, I can do a good service by bringing them over into English. And yet, even among that pool, I have my favourites and less favourites. The best translations are of those poems that made the translators jealous upon first reading them in the original — 'Why couldn't I come up with that?' So they do the next best thing and recreate the work that fascinates them in the target language. That's the case of every poem in this collection, regardless of the quality of the translation. In the original Polish, they all hit me, hard.

And that's another reason why I wouldn't do the general casting call to one and all Polish poets. Because then I'd have to reject some of them, too, and run the risk of bruising their feelings. And poets, like dogs and translators, are people too.

Most of my translations are fronted with an analytic, critical introduction, with close readings of the works I've translated, comparisons to other authors, and a general literary and historical context that, I hope, allows the reader a better insight into the text that he or she is approaching for the first time. I am not doing that with *150 Poems from Poland*. In line with my premise of having the anthology written by the poets, in their own voices, I will eschew even an 'objective' consideration of their poems and essays here, as such a thing, too, would be to direct the reader, to impose my opinions on him or her, to interpose myself between him or her and the poets in question. So I'll end this explanation here and let the poets take over themselves, speaking in their own voices.

Aha. The fact of there being 178, not 150, poems in *150 Poems from Poland* is due, primarily, to the above-mentioned tweaking of the parameters when I decided to accept everything that the poets sent me. If everything had gone along according to the original design of ten poems each, there would be only ninety poems. Because of the broadening of the scheme, the anthology grew by nearly 100%, with eighty-eight more poems added.

What is more, some of them are my own. I say above that I am 'a translator, not a poet', and I say this for reasons that I explain in my own essay, appended to the end of my own section. How do I qualify? Well, despite what I say above, I am a poet after all, according to the definition so aptly formulated by both Andrzej Kotański and Krzysztof Koehler, in that I have been known to make the effort of noting down the inspiration that comes to all of us from time to time. And these 'poetic notes' have been published over the years in five collections: three in English (*Beast, Diet of Nails, Chanameed*) and two in Polish (*Hallo Sztokholm, Skowycik*). I am also Polish by ethnicity (with a good measure of Slovak tossed in) and citizenship. Is it amour-propre that has me include my own work as the supernumerary, tenth poet, in this anthology? I won't deny it, if so accused. Still, as a reader, I think it's interesting when the translator, who has also published original poetry, introduces himself to the reader as a poet along with the poets he is translating. (If you don't happen to agree, you don't need to read them; this is one reason why they're set at the end.)

All of my poems appearing here were first published in the two of my books that were brought out in Poland, with one or two exceptions of completely new ones, destined for a third collection which, in all probability, will not see the light of day. For with last year's *Skowycik*, I think I've come to the end of writing poetry myself. I mentioned this to one of my friends (included here) over a beer at the Teatralna café in Kraków. He responded, 'No more poetry? What? You planning on kicking the bucket?' God forbid! But, although more than one of the poets found here would not agree with me, poetry is a young man's game, and I'm now past sixty... So this is probably it for me, as a poet. As the immortal Morrissey puts it in 'Disappointed', 'This is the last song I will ever sing' (hurrah! in the background). But who knows? As the song goes on, 'Ah no, I've changed my mind again' (groans in the background). So we'll see. In any case, Reader, I hope you enjoy *150* [178] *Poems from Poland*. That you'll read it through. And keep it. And want to read it again. And buy it again when you loan it out and the person you loan it to falls in love with it and doesn't give it back. And so on. Peace.

Port St Lucie, 14 January, 2025

Eligiusz Dymowski

CONCERNING THE MAN WHO NEVER FOUND HIMSELF

The man
who never found himself
—is dead

Yesterday he left a note:

'I know that nothing's
keeping me here'

and departed through the window

ROOMS

There are no empty walls
in the chambers of my heart
I have hung them with
threads of the imagination
so that those who sometimes enter
should not be frightened

'I GAVE BIRTH TO THE SON'

I gave birth to the Son
—of God—
as a mother I am happy
but my heart trembles in fear
despite the Angel's assurance
Fear not Mary
You have been set apart by grace

but after all every mother
fears for her child

Who will he become
the one that I—simple girl from Nazareth
gave unto the world

and in my hands I hold my tears
I—who gave birth to the Son
—of God—

Eligiusz Dymowski

A WOMAN, BY RENOIR

You needn't take off your hat
I'll paint you just so
adding only a smile
so that no one should know
the suffering you've given birth to
in your heart
suffering sufficient for several nights
before at last you fall asleep

LETTER TO A FRIEND IN THE WEST

Sorry. It's been a while since I've written.
I'm sure you've heard—there've been some big changes
    round here.
But who cares?
life has narrowed
to the daily inspection of one's wallet
and dread of the future...
The churches still stand
though ever more crows perch on the roofs.
Priests get sad too—
our hearts aren't made of stone,
and everyone is looking at one's hands.
You see!
We must ever be on the road to Democracy,
but the road is a long one,
and the best students in the class
have turned out stubborn.
And so day after day rolls by,
night after night, even the sun gets up late.
People are waiting on a miracle.
Forgive me! That's all I have.
. . . .
PS
I reckon that
your streets are still being swept
by professors from the East?

Mazovia, Summer 1993

Eligiusz Dymowski   17

I DON'T KNOW

i don't know
how many hours must be wept through
along one's daily path

i don't know
how wide one's arms must be stretched
for the cross to fit

i don't know
if truth is carved in stone
suffering for sure

i don't know
why love and death
are so inseparable

i don't know
when the sun will be snuffed
and the earth burst into flame

i don't know

me — doubting Thomas
am astounded still I sense
Thy hand stretched forth towards the blind man

JOB'S VISION

scrape the scales from your eyes
light harms not
the blind

fire and water
lose not their force
in the arms of eternity

and no trial
lasts longer
than life

just keep on
being
stronger
than yourself

Metaponte, in December 1998

THE HOST

Seemingly —
        small
swelling with lightness
and
entirely God

WHEN A POET DIES

In memoriam Fr Jan Twardowski

When a poet dies
Don't join the funeral cortège
gloomily
because Heaven's spread wide its arms

When a poet dies
beat loud drumrolls
let them awaken the hope
contained in prayers
of Happiness

When a poet dies
only then does life
really awaken
in his poems

Kraków, the Azores, January 2006

WINDOW WITH A VIEW ON VESUVIUS

At night the Bay of Naples
looks like a glowing crater
the lights flowing like lava
bring to mind the last days of Pompeii

Annihilation always arrives
when it's least expected

The excellent wine
dulls the senses of the gods
engaged in the ritual dance
of sin and death

The skeletons of human bodies
stripped of their nudity
no longer arouse revulsion or compassion

What was supposed unto dust to return
has returned unto the dust

Poseidon's begun another war
people have come to believe in their own divinity
placing upon their brows the crown of pride

Only He who created the universe
is silent
and shall be until the final explosion
of Apocalypse

MY FRIEND THE CAT

For my Father, on his name-day

my cat
whose dainty name is Cocaine
is not superstitious in the least
he crosses the street calmly
he never claws his way up a tree without some good reason
he has nothing to do with tarot cards
or interpreting hands of solitaire

while I'm reading my breviary
he swipes his paws at the colourful ribbons
and when he hears the Angelus bell ring
he beats out the time with his tail against the chair
peering at me intently
with his feline eyes

what's more he adores blazers
(especially tweed blazers)
when I lay them on my bed
he penetrates each sleeve
as if he were playing hide and seek

in the evening when I put on my pyjamas
he begins a crazy dance in a joyful trance sensing
that he won't be left alone now for long hours

just like me my cat
clumsily stretches out his paws to the sky
to beg his lord
for a bowl of food
to provide strength for the ordinary daily grind

how can one not raise thanks to God
for providing man
with nine such happy lives

Kraków 9 December 2009

Eligiusz Dymowski   23

THE BIRTH OF BEAUTY,
or THE FIRST BEDAZZLEMENT

that woman with the white rose
is neither saint nor sinner

that woman with the white rose
talks to God in her own way

, about you

if you want to do something for her
give her love

and you'll see how her eyes get slowly dazzled
by happiness

DON COGITO'S HOLY WEEK

Be watchful —when the signal lamp flares on the summit —
get up and go.

—Zbigniew Herbert

You shall be judged by infidel and hypocrite
for communing too familiarly with Truth.

They will set up your gibbet in a public place,
so as to expectorate their bile
proclaiming a sham triumph
worth no more than a fistful of sand.

Roosters will crow summoning judases
and herods will run away in solitary panic
when the people despised spread wide the city gates.

But you, go—pay no heed—with head held high
You, Wisdom brought low on the summit of Golgotha!

THE MONASTERY OF ST GEORGE, WADI AL-KILT

in the evening in prayerful silence
the monks exit the church

their long beards
like the wings of angels
are ennobled by the gloom

the hour of rest approaches
the hour of reclining upon the Lord's bosom

following the Last Supper
no one wants to be
judas

for after all it's long been common knowledge
that the world is not saved
piecemeal

CONSIDERING MARIAN KOŁODZIEJ'S PAINTINGS AT HARMĘŻE

The heavens, sealed tight in dark clouds
awaken the demons of war. Their skeletons, like the
    chimneys of crematoria,
constantly loom in dread above millions of innocent beings.
If ever Hell is born here on the earth,
your voice must be heard by the confessors of evil. It's
    not for them
that the sun's gone black, burying in famine-sunken
    cheeks all hope of a peaceful rest.

You returned to a land accursed, not as lord and ruler,
    but as witness.
This hurts more than the barbed wire binding human ash.
History will never be just until it grapples with truth.
Memory, wounded all over by you, has bit into
the paper and burrows deep, image after image,
so that Death, so sure of herself and cruel, should no
    longer devour anyone.

Here struggle a demon and an angel over which of them
    will be first
to tear away the curtain of cruelties and mock the
    self-satisfied onlookers.
But humanity does not end at this crime scene,
for the remnants of human dignity remain, and the cry
    from the abyss:
Requiescat in pace!

Eligiusz Dymowski   27

A WOMAN IN BLACK POSES FOR HER PORTRAIT

liberated from guilt a hundred times over
lightly she submerges herself in fall
storing in her memory the image
of seagulls dancing
above the waves of the agitated sea
her narrowed eyes
speak more right now of happiness
than you think

'SYLVIA PLATH KNOWS'

The moon has nothing to be sad about.

— Sylvia Plath

Sylvia Plath knows now
that she won't write another poem

she sets aside the empty sheet of paper
like an unfulfilled love
for better days

before the sun rises
she'll still have time
to cry down a red rain
upon the earth cracked with pain
so as once again to become dust

Eligiusz Dymowski

ON THE BANKS OF THE NIEWIAŻA

For Czesław Miłosz

The lazy current of the river brings recollections of childhood.
And although happiness is not dependent on its length,
the river still moves and delights the heart.

For here it all began and still endures. The poet shall write:
Wherever I've wandered, whatever the continent,
I've always stood facing the River.

Still in the meanders and thickets of memory
the spirits of the dead return at night
to remind the living of their existence.

Eyes fixed upon the dark ribbon of water,
in silence we give thanks to God for the day
on which He created both the river and us.

Szetejnie, 2018

MADAME BOVARY, BEFORE DEPARTURE

write a poem
—she said, taking a drag on her cigarette—
write it for me
I no longer want
to share words and yearnings
with the tears
of other women
just remember
eternity must be just

'LEDA AND THE SWAN'
ACCORDING TO GUSTAVE MOREAU

For you I'll give birth to love
just give me time
to get used to the pain
after the loss of the whiteness
of my dreams
it doesn't matter anymore
what colour
we paint the walls

POETRY:
THE WATCHFUL EYE OF THE CYCLOPS

Will the twenty-first century deprive humans of their desire for beauty? Will that, which once constituted our spiritual foundations, be seen as something no longer necessary to anyone? Mass culture, being the force that it is, strikes at the most sensitive string of the human imagination, especially in our seeing 'farther and deeper'. The spiritual indolence of the world has become something of a basic cult in contemporary civilisation, where man, fed on mealy grits, becomes what he eats. Long ago, Czesław Miłosz meditated on this very thing, writing, 'It is the great mystery of our times—how can people—great masses of people—be provided with books that would be simultaneously legible and comprehensible, without appealing to the worst of tastes?' Can it really be that so-called high culture and art are seen as a threat to the freedom of industrial society?

Each and every expectation bears within it an element of insecurity and suffering. And in that climate, the consciously creative artist is at home. This is especially true of the poet. Currently, his influence is limited—more or less distinctly—to the minimum, as far as the reality that surrounds us is concerned. Testimony to this fact is provided by the small print runs of volumes of poetry, the ever-shrinking interest of the mass consumer in poetry recitals and the very reading of poetry, which in the general understanding of people has become illegible, incomprehensible, and impractical. The poet has ceased to be the voice of a generation in rebellion—a generation, the content of whose lives in our day and age is provided by the omnipresent social media, whereby just about all human desires are satisfied and all spiritual ailments cured.

And so where is the poet to find a place for himself, and for poetry, in the thickets of such bitter truths? Are they still really necessary to anyone? And what is poetical inspiration in the face of the ever more dominant voice of artificial intelligence? But let us not allow ourselves to be overcome with pessimism. As Jean Cocteau tells us, 'Poetry is indispensable. If only I knew why!' And it is along just such a path, not fully comprehensible to the reason, that man must tread to the very end.

Just as like every artist, the poet is — and should remain — a person of strong passions and firm convictions, distant from all rash canonisations and brittle pedestals. The poet is the spirit of his time. It is he, or she, who best understands the needs of the heart, its anxieties, and the storms of its desires. It is for this reason that he must scrape away from his imagination all accumulated grime that, like chaff, fouls the grain, saps the strength, and blurs the form of the real image. The poem he creates must find its balance between the abstract and the concrete, between thought and image, between emotion and prudence. Only then can it become a load-bearing support for the spiritual imagination and an authentic motor of courageous action and choice. Only then will it be capable of describing states of consciousness with mathematical precision, without which pure abstraction becomes truly alien, cruel, and incomprehensible.

Poetry is also a matter of style, and style — once more I return to Miłosz — 'is man'. That is, his manner of thinking, behaviour, his choices, and his possibilities. We learn of this through careful observation of our surroundings whether we are poets or receptors of poetry. And so poetry is strongly rooted in its time, its given moment, just as intrinsically as birth and death. It is time and the style of that time upon which depend our consciousness and our poetic inspiration, unburdened by any unnecessary decorations and empty metaphors, so as to avoid becoming a mealy craft.

Many of my favourite poets and creators have trod just such a path. Consequent in their choices and strong in defeat. Consciously moving against the current of loud, garish — and passing — fads. Faithful to their inspirations, their vocation; conscious of the fact that not everyone will accord them respect or tip a hat to them. And yet they endured to the end. Let me mention just a few here, such as Norwid, Eliot, Herbert, and Świrszczyńska — just a few, as the list might certainly be much longer and multi-sectional.

Poetry is the watchful eye of the Cyclops. The feverish rise of poetic abstractions, which can be noted over the last few decades, adds little new to true poetry. In this garden, it can be easy to mistake weeds for edible plants. And yet everyone makes his or her own choice. This goes on constantly: between truth and falsehood, between good and evil. Yet there always remains time for deeper reflections and original, well-thought-out opinions, which in just such a manner bear witness to our style and taste in recognising and understanding the essence of true beauty.

ELIGIUSZ DYMOWSKI was born on 4 July, 1965, in Sanniki, in central Poland. A Franciscan priest, he is a theologian, a poet, and a literary critic. He studied at the Theological Institute of the Missionary Fathers in Kraków, as well as at the Lateran University in Rome, obtaining his doctorate in 2001 at the Papal Academy of Theology in Kraków. In 1994, a stipend from the French Embassy to the Holy See in Rome permitted him to study at the Catholic University in Lyon. He served as a parish priest in Pińczów and at Somma Vesuviana near Naples. Between the years 1999 and 2005, he was rector of the Higher Seminary of the Franciscan Fathers in Kraków–Bronowice Wielkie. At present, he is the superior and rector of the Franciscan parish in Kraków–Bronowice Wielkie. Besides engaging in writing and research, he teaches. He is a member of the Polish Theological Society, the European Society of Culture, the Association of Polish Writers, and the Academia Europaea Sarbieviana. He is the author of theological and literary works, having brought out seventeen volumes since his debut in 1987. His poems have been translated into many languages and may be found in both Polish and foreign-language anthologies. In 2013, he was awarded the Świętokrzyski Gustaw Literary Award in Kielce (literary criticism and poetry). In 2017, he was awarded the Order of Merit for Service to Polish Culture by the Polish Ministry of Culture and National Heritage; in 2020, the Naji Naaman Literary Prize (Prix de créativité) in Lebanon; and in 2021, the Honoris Gratia medal was presented him by the President of Kraków, where he resides.

Michał Zabłocki

AT THE W. INTERNATIONAL AIRPORT

At the W. International Airport
I'm waiting for a flight
to transport me to L.

In a few hours I'll land
in the midst of something
that doesn't concern me at all.

I will look at many splendid things,
which will make no impression on me
whatsoever.

I will sit in a few places
to which I'm completely indifferent
hawking my doubtful knowledge
at a steep price
knowledge of things for which
I myself wouldn't give a wooden nickel.

I don't know when it all
began
and I don't know how long it'll last.

Some people call it life.

Michał Zabłocki   39

TWO PROPOSALS OF DARING REBELLION
IN LINE WITH YOUR HUMBLE CAPABILITIES
(A PRACTICAL GUIDE FOR YOUNG POETS)

And so, if you really must, try this:
Approach the wall.
Strike it with your head.
Now or never.
Let's go!
Gather all your august intentions
and widespread ambitions
in one point in the centre of your brow.
O unicorn, you symbol of the void,
whap your head
against the clean plane of whitewashed cement.
Rebel against the unlimited strength
of rebar in poured concrete.
And do what has heretofore been impossible:
break on through to the other side,
remaining audaciously alive!

Or even better—
—jump out the window
and levitate outside the second floor
(having leapt from the eighth);
flap your arms
and descend, delicately, like a silken scarf
down onto the monstrously alluring
black of the asphalt.

Ouch! So hot!
In such a swelter you'll jump barefoot?

STREETWALKER

That lady sitting there
hatted
benchly streetified
musicalised from the rear
by a band
gets up (but she was sitting down)
sits down (but she was standing up)
disassembles herself fleshly
(but only eyewitnessly)

And yet she's just now market-squared
un-streetified having
effectively hand(l)ed round her
(well-worn)
queans to any old jack

Now slithers (titters, tilts'er
tits) forward (and back)
and there on the bench—flitters
(her eyes, sitting while)
somebody shifts (hips) her
fur(ther on)

And suddenly:
unhatted!
and here, and there,
and everywhere at once
I gape, I goggle
P'raps rude? What?
now (without that hat)
she's totally nude

I hesitate
(hanging, dangling)
and what if I were to
unhitch and attach
(shift)
all that elaborate
behatted

Michał Zabłocki   41

marketsquared
streetwalker
dot all the ises and areses

And then bend
(drop)
place
(in pocket)
and leave

FROM AN ANCIENT POEM
(THE FRAGMENT THAT SURVIVES)

Look, my wound [seeps]
   ...disreputable misdeeds
   on a day so joyful...

The child of his [mother]...
   ...the viper.
   ...long since the days had passed...
   ...and life, is it worth living...

Advise [aid me], answer the...
   ...for sense is in forgetfulness...
   ...and only time heals [steals?]...

WORDS OF ADVICE GIVEN BY THE YOUNG POLISH POET MICHAŁ ZABŁOCKI TO THE LATE ITALIAN POET EUGENIO MONTALE FOLLOWING HIS READING OF THE POEM BY THE RECENTLY DEPARTED RUSSIAN AND AMERICAN POET JOSIF BRODSKY ENTITLED 'IN THE SHADOW OF DANTE' (ANOTHER ITALIAN POET LIKEWISE DEFUNCT)

Thin and bloodless metaphors
anaemic allusive schemes
Montale will never help you soar
above Dante the Florentine.

Good Lord but don't take that to mean
You're as ignorant as one can get
(like me) but reading this, I ween
It'll help you to forget.

MISTAKEN WORDS

Mistaken words
Make up the wonder
Of the verse.

Mistaken people
Make up the wonder
Of the universe.

PONT DES ARTS

We Mick the First
King of Poland Greece and France
Have led our hosts
In triumph
Through the Pont des Arts in Paris
In anticipation whereof a large number
Of African carvings of natural proportions
Were set up in homage by that strange continent
For the Polish Greek and French nations
We ourselves on behalf of our court and army
Here express our gratitude to the African continent
For its celebration of our triumph
With the works of art which we passed by in wonder and
    confusion
May this particular gesture
Plant an iron seed
That when germinating shall wind about
Our nations binding them in a firm embrace

Regardless of content, regardless of form

RECALLING TILOS

There is no stele
There is no tomb
No one here remembers You at all

Erinna Erinna
Once lived here
She owned four goats
And died last Thursday

Here look look here her house stood here
A complete ruin since antiquity
We'd need to excavate the garden wall
While that wild fig of hers still bears fruit

Michał Zabłocki

THE ANCIENTS

The ancients are no one to sneeze at
They made nothing out of plastic
They rejected automobiles in time
They untelephoned their cities

And yet they had so much to fix:
They had to cleanse the filthy seas
Reduce the number of people
And liquidate the garbage dumps

People took notice of their skills
Began to give the ancients jobs
Ever more exalted posts
In administration, main offices

Importing them from far away
Signing them to contracts eternal
The ancients never had it so
Good as they have it here and now

THRENODY FOR A POET

Only when it's all over
Will someone be found
Who will come up
Slap the shoulder
And say:
You weren't bad
Really not bad at all
Too bad you didn't die earlier

You would have been famous
Made a career
But thus?
You got in the way
Took up space
You had no influential friends
By living long
You gave them enough rope
To hang you with

And now
You can only count
On belated and dubious riflers
So make sure to mark your grave well

You're buried in the farthest row
To the left
Right at the wall

Farther on
Over there
No one's buried but suicides.

Michał Zabłocki   49

SEVEN SEALS

Seven seals were affixed and the tome was sealed on the
last page
The letters thickly filled the area set aside for their content
No space was lacking nor was any left over for any additions
Everything took place on the previously determined day,
the hour planned upon
But to some it seems that it might have been different
That so many errors might have been avoided
That the love and the hatred could have been more
unconditional
Chapter sixteen might have been retarded or speeded up
The beginning simplified the end complicated
Contrary to what is written there
To others it seems that in the middle of the introduction
A logically thinking person might already intimate the end
In connection with which he entered the conspiracy imper-
sonated the culprit
Killed the hero himself and hid him in the grotto
So the tome was a fiction of rather poor quality
In which the characters act in a criminal manner
And for God's sake it's only a fairy story for loony oldsters
Sitting on their pillars in the middle of the desert

CIRCUS MAXIMUS

Here is the real Circus Maximus
When we're racing for arguments
With the emperor gazing down at us from the Palatine
Sighing at the idiocy of his charioteers
These words of ours are like rickety nags
Hardly able to budge the chariot
To say nothing of competing for a real golden chaplet
The ticket to eternal honours
Our chariots tilt over at each turn
While our rivals are far ahead on the straightaway
The only thing that's left us are these pitiful quarrels
About who shall deign to bear the shame of losing
While the whole arena's so shaking from the laughter
That even the stands are collapsing
The public flail about in puddles of rain
Three hundred thousand people croaking like frogs
And in his palace Caesar is red with shame

Michał Zabłocki   51

QUINTUS, TO SEPTIMUS

My dear Septimus
I'm writing to You in a private matter, as I know you won't
    just bat me aside
Just imagine what's happened
You know me well enough and I needn't remind you of
    ancient histories
Travelling from province to province in the service of the
    emperor
In essence, I've always been alone
Married in Rome as you remember well I left the city alone
Claudia Tarquinia is to blame, as she refused to leave the
    court on my behalf
I demanded a divorce and got one
It seemed to me that she was suffering a morbid case of
    civilisation
And that somewhere beyond Rome I'd find my life partner
But the same thing always happened
As soon as I'd meet someone I'd have to go away
And they always had more important things to do:
A family an inheritance or their own gods whom they refused
    to abandon
Each time disillusioned I left alone again
Until at last I lost all hope of any positive outcome of events
The world is sick, dear Septimus
You of all people don't need to be convinced of that
But just think what happened lately
Our boats anchored in Philippi
An Italian colony that, so I almost felt as if I were in Rome
And letters from the world entire began to catch up to me
And just imagine my wonder when I opened seven long
    letters
Sent by women from the most divers provinces
Not excepting good old honest Tarquinia
And all of them writing the same thing with minor variations:
I'm ready to follow you
What do you make of that, sweet Septimus?
Just don't write anything along the order of:

Tell each one of them to come
Hightailing it yourself for northern Gaul
Even though that might be the best thing to do

SEPTIMUS, TO QUINTUS

My dear Quintus
In reply to your letter
Which is moving proof of the trust you hold me in
But beyond that an interesting case study of the times we
    live in
Allow me to remind you of Papias' book on womankind
Which we discussed together some twenty-five years ago
Enthralled at the time with the cult of Mother Earth
With some serious reserve we accepted his statements
Which with the passage of time are worth underscoring
The cult of birthing fertility and in general everything asso-
    ciated with nature
Must be considered from the perspective of the health of
    soma and perhaps even *psyche*
Such a cult must never obscure the cult of the high heavens
In other words, everything that is better more distant and
    inscrutable
Great ideals have always been are and shall be beyond the
    reach of healthy beasts
And have never even crossed the minds of the most fertile
    among them
If the body did not go hand in hand with spirit we as Romans
Would never have taken half the world under our control
Should a man depart and a woman choose not to follow him
That is very well and indeed that's how it should be
Because gold is proven in very hot vessels
The ore indeed is noble but must be scoured by the fire
And it seems that in the end experience has taught those
    women many things about life
And for that reason they're now willing to drop everything
    and follow you
But there are two details that prove it's all in vain
Firstly time passes and never returns
You were so inclined to give each of them a chance
Now as you have been disappointed it's hard to speak of
    feelings
Secondly it's not about moving on but rather enduring

Along with you they'd have to bow before the gods of the
    high heavens
And that I guarantee you none of them are prepared to do
They only wish to reacquire the chance they lost
But at the bottom of it all they have not changed
They raise no daily prayers for their own betterment
Nor do they make an examination of conscience concerning
    their deeds
As our philosophers encourage us to do
But rather, they are fighting for the peace they find
When they recall that you were once close to them
Or perhaps I'm mistaken my dear Quintus?
I'd very much like to discuss good old Papias with you again
Strolling over the Quirinale
For unfortunately Africa is very sparse in cultivated men
And here there are only petty local gods

GIRLS

Seventy two young Jewish girls
Nervous and chattering
Stood facing me
In the line to the loo
At a petrol station
In central Poland
They fixed their eyes on me
Like burning torches
Precisely aimed
At every native
Every pale-faced fruit
Forbidden by the Bible of rules
I felt quite clearly on my cheeks
The hot blast of the desert
Spooked
As if I were a full-blooded Arab
I hid myself before the blitz
Of a foreign junket to Auschwitz

IN THIS DIVE

In this dive they make you pay first
They've had too many bad experiences
They won't pour you a tea without a fiver
You order but the waitress waits
Who knows what she's waiting for
But at last you get it
And then comes the key moment
Something inside you tells you you've been had
That first you're supposed to get the goods and then you pay
So you start to dicker
You put down two złote and say You'll get the rest later
The waitress pours some hot water but she won't hand it over
Not until you add another złoty
The last two wander from hand to hand
Left the cash register right the bag to be steeped
But she's not sure that you have a coin in your fist
And you're not sure that you'll get the taste you're after
It's a battle of wills Open your fist You first
You struggle like that a good while
But in the end madame is stared down
She tosses the teabag on the counter and withdraws from
    the bar weeping:
What a nightmare of a country in which two people can't
    trust one another
You think the same thing
You fling the two-złote coin and crack the mirror behind
    the bar
Before getting up in a huff and going out
What a nightmare of a country

Michał Zabłocki   57

WHO AM I

Who am I?
I asked my mama just for fun
and that's why this production was to be called Sonbrother
But isn't
Nobody'd want to know
What's up with that Sonbrother
What a strange title—they'd say—I'm not buying that
That's exactly what they'd say—I'm not shelling out
40 złoty for any Sonbrother
Now for Janowska, for Janowska sure
because I know her from TV and the colour inserts

Who am I?
I asked my mama to test her intelligence
Because after all we know
that people who have Alzheimer's can't recognise their own
so I guess I don't have to explain that anymore to anyone

Who am I?
I asked my mama and I heard her hesitate
a very loud hesitation
like the rapping of a metronome
I know—I don't, I know—I don't
Just the same as I
when someone I haven't seen for long approaches
I know—I don't, I know—I don't
And the metronome raps
after a while the person waiting gets offended
I'm not offended mama
we didn't know one another well
not well enough by far

Who am I?
Son? Husband? Friend? Lover? Minister?
Michał? Staś? Wojtek? Józek? Marek? Artur?
And mama replies:
You're Witek
your second name is Michał

Good, I thought
But who's this Witek?
Witek's a boy I knew in the uprising.
And Michał?
Michał's my husband

Who am I?
Because if Witek's a boyfriend and Michał's a husband
well, tough, I'll be one and the other at the same time
And mama: well it's obvious
first you were my friend, and only later my husband

Who am I?
Because I still have doubts
wasn't that friend of yours named Zbyszek?
His name was Zbyszek
And Witek
no, not Witek
Witek's name was Zbyszek?
Stop talking nonsense
All right, but who's that Witek?
Witek's dead
So not me?
It's you
So I'm not alive
So to speak

Who am I?
Because your husband's name is Wojtek
Wojtek? That's news to me
You don't know Wojtek?
I do
Who is Wojtek?
Wojtek's my husband
How do you know?
You just told me

Who am I?
Since Wojtek's your husband, who might Michał be?
Stop tormenting me
You want something sweet?

Michał Zabłocki   59

I didn't have a bite all day long
You just had dinner
I had neither dinner nor breakfast
You want something to eat?
Maybe so, maybe no, and Michał's my son

Who am I?
Living son and dead brother?
Michał and Witek?
Yeah. You're the sonbrother
I'm the sonbrother?
You're the sonbrother

THIS MOMENT

My father's not dying every day
at least for a certain while

But then yeah
at seven twenty three exactly
day after day
until the end of the world
he'll be taking a quick gasp
of one more breath of air
from a now forbidden reserve
from a completely empty supply

As if he wanted to make sure
that he's done everything
and hasn't overlooked a single chance
that he did his duty well

And we glance at one another helplessly
closing heavy eyelids
to solemnise the moment
the little piece of death
that lives in us

Michał Zabłocki

ARS POETICA

I don't know if I'm capable of expressing my *ars poetica* in a single, coherent, and somewhat accessible text. I've been writing now for some forty years, and my poetics have undergone so many metamorphoses, that I'm sure I would not be able to recognise those of the young boy who began his adventure with poetry in the 1980s. But one thing has remained unchanged from the start: I've always worked a lot, as I continue to do. I also throw a lot away, set a lot aside, destroy a lot. Writing is a part of my daily life. A manner of thinking. An ordering of the world. I also try to get that across to people who don't write themselves. Encouraging them to give it a go. Because writing changes one's life. Changes one's perspective. Changes reality—both interior and exterior reality. It changes everything. The well-grasped thought is capable of endowing all existence with meaning, of slaying every depression, indicating new goals. Without writing, everything erodes and devolves into chaos. When I am set upon by irritation, I know that I must return to it; that I've neglected it, and myself, for too long. In the history of my varied approaches to the writing process, several basic ones might be distinguished. Writing at night. Writing in the morning. Writing until noon; writing after noon. And writing in the evening. Am I stating something obvious? For sure. But the implications of these approaches aren't so obvious after all. Writing at night is compulsive writing, a grasping at a floatation device, sleepy, almost half-conscious writing. Morning writing is bright, certain, trusting in order and faithful to beginnings, automatic, swift. Writing before noon is professional writing: precise, thought out, and concentrated, realised especially—though not exclusively—when one is working on a commission and the course of one's life is stabilised and subjected to a single goal. Writing in the afternoon is melancholic, emotive, writing that rises above the surface of the world. Writing in the evening is a summary, an arrival at *pointes*, something concrete, sometimes even shallow—additional. Many other orders might be imposed on top of all these. For example, the order of impulses:

from one's core, from one's head, from experience. Or an order of challenges: from inner need—according to one's plan—on commission. It's hard to state which is the surest path to success and what's worthy of raising to the level of a confession of poetic faith. I'm constantly wavering, in an eternal search of new wellsprings of writing. I also like to set myself new tasks, to think up new objectives. None of my books ever came about according to prior rules thought up for subsequent exploitation. I've written for the stage, and I've written on the stage. I've written on the Internet and for the Internet. I've blogged and chatted. I've projected poems on the walls of buildings in the nighttime and published twenty traditional paper books. I've written as an individual and as part of a group. I'm the author of hundreds of songs, of which only a few have been sung; not many of these, but some rather well-known ones, constitute the basis of my financial upkeep. I've never worked in any profession other than writing, with the exception of an episode as a director, which lasted only a few years. I've been disappointed by all other realities and all other professions have let me down—professions I aimed at, for which I trained. And so with a clear conscience, I can state that I am a writer, professionally speaking, and that everything I've ever done in life has been subordinated to writing. Except life itself. For I strive not to make writing my life. I strive rather to write about life. But that's something different, something quite, quite different.

MICHAŁ ZABŁOCKI is an atypical poet. Along with having published twenty traditional volumes of poetry, he has been active in electronic publication on the Internet since 2000, he projects poems on public buildings at night, and appears in a literary cabaret. Lately, he has been performing his poems and songs live as Zabłocki Osobiście [Zabłocki Personally]. Each of these endeavours is a pretext for his constant experimentation and untiring search for new creative methods and varied literary conventions. He is a well-known author of songs, having won awards in this discipline, including first prize in the Muzyczna Jedynka competition of Polish Radio One in 1993. In 2018, he was awarded the bronze Gloria Artis medal by the Ministry of Culture of the Republic of Poland, and in 2021, the City of Kraków Prize for Cultural Achievements. The son of well-known parents, the television and film star Alina Janowska and Olympic champion fencer Wojciech Zabłocki, he published two volumes of poetry in honour of them: *Janowska* (2017) and *Ojcze nasz* [Our Father, 2022]. The last two poems in our selection come from these books. He is president of the Kraków branch of the Association of Polish Writers (SPP).

Adriana Szymańska

THE NOTEBOOK OF EXISTENCE

The passing of another day. Warm, sunny,
in the joyful chatter of sparrows.
Time is leafing through the pages of the well-worn notebook
    of existence.
Sewn together by the hand divine, in our hands
it falls into elementary sections. Separate:
the atoms of good and evil, of joy and pain. In this notebook
it's difficult to find one's ultimate moment.
Here, where your life's chronicle opens
into incomprehension, any sort of trifle can snag you, hold
    you up:
a cup of steaming coffee, the wagging of a dog's tail,
a phone call from a friend. These are your good moments.
Sadness sinks a cat's claw into you,
pricking your index finger to blood. Dizziness,
a lonely evening.
The distance from your steps to the garden
and the path in the woods suddenly becomes insurmountable.
But the notebook of existence turns a new page of day,
to once more write you into the pulsing current of minutes,
hours. Months? When you ask about years, time folds the page
like a paper airplane. It'll fly as far as the breath of God
    carries it.

Pułtusk, 13/14 June 2021

A CONFESSION

The trumpet from the town hall tower blares noon;
the bell from the church answers with the Angelus.
The aerial duet swirls aloft
like a pair of doves ascending to the clouds.
The heels of passersby rap out on the market-square cobbles
a rhythmic tattoo in accompaniment.
The windowpanes of the old buildings flash like eyes wide-open.
I'd like to dance on a nearby roof
along with the sparrows that flutter there.
Because I'm unable to renounce my love
for this world, with its crown of mist above the trees
of the park and the age-old battlements of the castle.
Crossing the bridge that spans the Narew,
I drop a birch-leaf onto the water's surface.
Let the current catch it and bear it
along with my confession of faith
into the bright misty haze.

Pułtusk, September 2022

A POEM FOR PIOTR SZEWC

Beauty enchanted in nature: in flowers,
birds, animals. At morning the six-legged spider
in my bathtub is like a star-shaped medal
pinned to a white scarf.
I reckon he got in last night through the window.
You asked me yesterday if I'd written anything new.
Yes, I'm writing a poem now thinking of you,
who also know our provincial secrets.
Titmice and sparrows on the balcony relate
the sonorous saga of their avian life. They are
like fluffy brooches in the still green leaves
of birch. It's near August, so all that blooms
and greens will remain a little while yet
in the fulness of its splendour.
The moon will soon wax full as well.
Its silver shield shone out on last night's sky
transforming the nearby roofs into mysterious mirrors
in which I sought the reflections of those souls
long departed hence.
Yes, Piotr, to live in delight is my task
for today. And tomorrow? Should you ask?
Only He, who loves me endlessly
might answer. But He'll remain silent
for as long as you'll be waiting
on my next poem.

31 July 2020

A CONFESSION WITH A SMILE

The abbess of an avian community
in the broad refuge of the garden.
That's how I see myself, spilling seed for the birds
through the windows at the east and west of the house
and hanging fatty morsels on the balcony.
In the foul winter weather the birds come visit me
from early morning, when my other life companions
are busied more with fending for themselves
than any wish to meet with me.
The garden of my house is my realm of joy
with little groups of birds for my court entourage.
Chirping, cooing, and cawing
they voice their gratitude for my largesse.
Each day I commence my journey
to the windows and garden paths, where
the hospitable feeders hang from the boughs of the trees.
How many avian souls have I saved? How many yet
will I save? And the birds recorded in my verse
will remain there ever alive and beautiful.
Someone, somewhere, sometime will perhaps award me
the Order of the Siskin Feather for my concern,
my praise of our fluffy winged
brethren. Although today I already bestow it upon myself.

In February 2024

MOUNT CARMEL

The longer I live, the more my world
crumbles to pieces. And among them
I must search for treasures.
One can go a long way
and yet see little. One can stand still
and become chosen. Then
there flutter to you the greatest minds
of all ages, ascending the mount of your
solitude. They knock at the wall of darkness
that surrounds you attempting to relate
what lies beyond. Today came knocking
Michelangelo. Yesterday, San Juan de la Cruz.
I couldn't understand much of their teachings
though each one came carrying his own gift
of endurance. Who shall come tomorrow, and the day after?
I peek through a chink in the wall and see
something like an organ of light. And next to it
Johann Sebastian Bach, pressing to his bosom the score
of his Cantatas. 'You see', he says, 'THERE
the angels are singing them. You too, take along
the best thing you've invented'.
I meditated a while on that before showing him
a smooth white stone I once found on the seashore.

2015

A SHORT TREATISE ON BEING ONESELF

For some one life is not enough
and so they seek out ways of multiplying it.
They pretend to be the heroes of books and films,
They've thought up reincarnation, life after life.
And yet this one and only life
that has been granted to us is a miracle
in and of itself, like a gift sent from eternity
through cosmic nebulae to these earthly gardens.
And no one's succeeded in ultimately penetrating
the sense and vocation of this life. Or to suss out
from myths and biblical parables what
will happen to us after death. Believing in God,
we hope for a return to paradise, loving
we trust in the righteousness of our path. When overcome
with resentment and anger we ask: what's it all for?
Even the greatest wisemen have doubted their own
conclusions, spooled from the clumsiness of reason.
I only know that I know nothing—this the slogan of one
    of them.
But maybe it would suffice to repeat with humility:
—Here I am, simply—me. I'm alive. Bathed in sunlight,
covered by the evening dusk, erring
on the side of caution, jumping the gun.
And this life is really all I have.
That with it I might glorify the world in being.

2 February 2023

RESCUE

I was born. And thus rescued
from eternal unbeing.
True enough, the snares of life more than once have tried
to pull me back into the black abyss
of the unmarked side of being, but He,
who sent me here, constantly multiplies in me signs
of endurance, so I can be myself—such as
I wish to be. And so: joyful, leaning out
the window each morning to greet other creatures,
also delighted with their being in this earthly flock.
At evening I send a smile towards the Unseen
and conjure those who—though unseen themselves—
are to me still like stars
shining forth one after the other in the night sky.
Father, mother, the man who rocked me
in his words—full of love—as well as
others even earlier, remembered from roads traversed
together. Yes, to be called to life,
that's like shining with the light reflected
from the fearless, ever void-conquering—Word.

In August 2022

RAPTURE

So many moments, words, so many dreams.
How does it all fit into one ephemeral life?
This world is one grand soaring altar
upon which we place all that abundance
of our deeds and expectations.
We know not what will happen tomorrow or next year,
and yet we greet each new day with a song.
To live means to grip tight this thread of wonder
hanging above the chasm of being here and now amidst
the unmarked paths of future happenings.
Walking straight ahead sometimes we forget
that we are a gift given to this world that awaits
the sowing of our hands and harvesting.
And still we must lift to the heavens
this unspotted offering of our forespent hearts
petitioning Him, who knows everything about us,
to bless them.

Pułtusk, 14/15 September 2022

THE BLUE SCARF

For Anna Piwkowska

To speak of the world — that one far away
stitched up with stars,
and this one, closest, eating fresh bread and butter
from the palm of your hand. The world
Is spreading wider: all the angels
have long ago flown out of all our dreams
for there, where no philosopher
cares to open his dubious eyes.
The world is tripping over a blade of grass
sprouting on the hill slope at dawn:
the word, although it sees other matters too
keeps that very grassblade in its shining eye.
This grassblade and that blue scarf — wrapped
around someone's heart so snugly
that, even should the whole universe catch fire
it — untouched — will save that heart
along with another. For — in all the wisdom
ever recorded and written down right now
with the plodding hand of that faith
that says love first, think later
of tears — the only measure of wisdom
is the sacred recollection of that
slender thread of omnipotence, when free,
we gave ourselves to someone — like a ray —
for eternal indissolubility.

2003

Adriana Szymańska

RADIANCE

Those bright provinces where I find myself
sometimes — like a bird, just passing through.
In daytime taking in the area
— from river to hilltop — that it might
defend me from the mist of loneliness.
At night sending whispers towards the farthest stars
that they might remain here — blazing, when I
return to town. Only here, amidst these orchards
does the cinnamon tiger of the noon
arch his back beneath the omniscient eye
of heaven. Only here the ruddy moon's a boat
in the clouds, where steep roofs flutter like sails
in the sprightly breeze. How many roads — forever mine,
though they've barely been brushed by my footfall?
Ruler of space — I stumble against a stone,
hardly able to count up the nooks of eternity
where I've overlooked the sleeping angels. For example
that meadow with its lonely maple seen from the passing train
as evening's about to fall: beyond it the house
with shingled porch and flashing windows — mightier
than light. But that sight surely never more brightly
shall burst in my eyes and the mystery shimmering
on the leaf of my soul shall be snuffed along with me.
So even here, where my sight reaches — from horizon
to horizon, I'm like a jackdaw on a branch,
cleaning his beak after an unexpected meal —
not knowing whom to thank for the largesse.

Sandomierz 2003

QUANDARIES

What is more, and what is less, important?
I know—I don't know. So much can I say,
when I listen to myself alone.
Endless quandaries—like a swing in motion.
Maybe I know too much, or maybe I'll never
discover how many generations must pass
before those who hate spread wide their arms,
and the envious too, in gestures of atonement?
When shall my faith move this mountain
of temporality, which I inhabit,
to the other side of existence? There
where neither hour, nor day, nor year means anything,
neither drought, nor downpour, nor beauty, nor fame,
but all one hears is that never-ending otherworldly hymn
　　　　　—of thanksgiving.

In September 2022

BIRTHDAY PARABLE

Eighty-one! Eighty-one!
—I repeat joyously every morning,
delighted at my still enduring life.
Adding one to eight, we arrive at nine.
Even the ancient philosophers and creators
of mythical narratives considered the number nine
a sign of fulness. And thus—perfection?
Fulness of life, of experiences, deeds,
of victories and failures. The mystical exaltation of the soul.
I reckon all from the beginning and I see
the failures vanish, as if at the touch
of a magic wand. Such a comforting vision.
It's marvellous to recall only that
which cast upon our days the golden glow
of immaculate yearning. Looking ahead
I see the glow still, which supports me
in my daily tasks. Cleaning, eating,
praying, resting, wandering about the streets
of my quarter amidst orchard trees and friendly
animals, I'm constantly smiling.
Smile—that's my advice for those who
see little ahead of themselves. In smiles there lies a power
that rescues from doubt, a salvific hope
that I wish myself and others. As the kite longs for rain, I
long to arrive at the finish. And Go Farther. For I believe
    that Farther On
—written with capital letters—lies the Smile Eternal
with which one day I'll greet from That Side
my existence. Sooner or later, maybe
just around the corner? I ask, because I like questions.
For in questions, after all, lie inevitable answers.

2024

PSALM, WITH A SMILE

Thanks be to You, Lord, for the heart
that so gaily dances in my bosom
at each meeting with You.
For You are in everything that You permit me
to love. These children, friends, dogs, cats, and birds,
bees, bumblebees, and crickets
ticking at nighttime like tiny watches.
These flowers, grasses, and trees in the garden,
the fields and woods with paths over which
so many times my feet have wandered.
The seas and rivers with the sparkling scales of waves
in which gulls and jet planes see their reflections.
The sun and the stars. These immense spaces
at which one need only glance to embrace
with tender thought and playful imagination.
Today I placed my heart inside a soap-bubble
dancing on the breeze, and painting upon it
my smile, I went on my way, farther
into that radiant blue. May it find its way
into Your hands, O Lord, when the proper time comes.

In September 2022

Adriana Szymańska

ANALOGY

One, two, three, five, nine, eighteen . . .
Counting the beats of one's heart at night is
like peeping at the stars winking in heaven:
you never know when you ought to stop.
And still and all this crazy pulse of mine
governs nothing but my individual person,
whereas the life of the stars is involved within
the history of the entire universe.
And yet I see a certain similarity: my heart
is a pulsar too, which, dying, flashes
unto the world beams of the poems it pulses out.

2010−2022

TRANSUBSTANTIATION

To write a poem is to remove a thorn from one's heart.
Or to liberate one's thought from an acute sadness.
To speak of oneself is like uprooting a tree
from sterile soil, transplanting it in fat black earth.
For pain and sadness are of a variable nature:
expressed, they scamper away from your thoughts, your
    feelings.
And then the act of transformation begins:
when the light of day scatters the darkness of night,
you effect the miracle of transubstantiation.
It's just like in the prayer: And the Word became flesh.
There are no imperfect prayers. All of them
are like long poems proclaiming love not of this world,
Not of this world, but of That, which you come to know
tramping stubbornly over this world's paths.
But if you tread carefully, perhaps in the end you'll stand
before the Light that shines from beyond the gate of Heaven.

1/2 January 2019

WHY DO I WRITE? AN ARS POETICA

I write because I believe in cognition, which is a manner of rescue. And so I believe in my own poetry and in all other poetry that fixes its eyes on the Absolute. I believe that thought and imagination are capable of penetrating the darkness. Darkness is ignorance, a lack of faith, hope, and love. The light of cognition, which penetrates the darknesses of evil and suffering, gives wings to the mind, allowing it to soar over the incomprehensibility of existence, above the abyss of death. Everyone experiences the burden of fate, which passes no person by, in his or her own manner. To be able to discover a goal for one's yearnings for freedom, despite being under the pressure of vital determinations, is a task cut to human measure.

In his *Journey to the End of Night*, Louis-Ferdinand Céline describes in such a laconic fashion the pressure of existence as it forms the individual identity: 'Perhaps it is this indeed that one searches for throughout one's life: just this, the greatest worry that might exist, in order to become oneself before death'. Perhaps, besides its compensatory functions, in my own intimate experience, poetry—by which I attempt to express both the lunacy of love and the torment of ephemerality, the terror of memory—plays the role of a guiding star leading me through the wilderness of the present moment. It is not so much an escape from the decrees of fate as it is a search for the meaning of suffering. Have I found my 'greatest worry' yet? Does there even exist some measure of resilience to metaphysical anxiety and the existential pain of separation, of loss? I know this one thing for sure, that there is no better vaccine against the salvo of inevitabilities of life than poetry. I'm alive, so I write poems. I find myself incapable of expressing myself any more exactly as far as this condition of mine is concerned.

I believe in love, which is the queen of all virtues. I believe that, even here and now, while I'm still alive, I'll come to know what love is, truly—already I almost do. I believe that when I lie dying, I will feel free of what was my guilt here, my faults and flaws in relation to myself and to others. Because as St John writes, 'For if our heart reprehend us, God is greater than our heart, and knoweth all things' (1 John 3:20). I write because I believe in the divine source of poetry. I believe in the wisdom of its intentions, in that saving, regenerative energy of the Word, which has been given to us so that we should love one another (in Him). And so I write poetry, because in poetry I can most effectively express my acceptance of the world. As I see it, my poems are above all an act of love in relation to the people I love, to animals, plants, to the whole world, the cosmos, to matter and the spirit of its Creator that suffuses it all. As I once wrote in the introduction to my *Poezje wybrane* [Selected Poems, 1987], 'My first poem was a prayer. So was the second, third, and the tenth. This was in my childhood, when the boundaries between truth and imagination are in flux, when faith and the object of adoration have not yet been separated by the blade of rationalism. At the time, my God existed for me really and truly as the highest measure, the omnipotent Being, omniscient and magnanimous. My childish, imagined God was the ideal partner, discovered once and for all time, Who satisfied the overarching instinct of communion'.

It was Simone Weil who taught me that watchfulness is a synonym for love. It is when I am watchful, vigilant, that I become a poet. For I believe in cognition, which, as a manner of rescue, also functions as a loving covenant with the world. Cognition, treated exclusively as an attempt at penetrating the mystery of existence by thinking, has posed tormenting problems to more than one philosopher. And it is in this that those who consider the knowledge won by poetry higher than the hypotheses of philosophy are correct. For the poet — even as he or she struggles painfully to arrive at his or her own vision of the world — experiences at least sometimes the comfort that arises from the epiphany that, all of a sudden, shines around him: as he (or she) discovers himself as an inalienable element of the cosmos, and comes to feel himself to be just as beautiful as every other creature. At most, the philosopher might confess, 'Here is the tragedy: the greatest graces of life become the source of suffering through the alienation to which they sentence us. For most people don't want to have anything to do with them, and sometimes even damn them. The greatest varieties of happiness bear within themselves this sadness: that they cannot be shared — nobody wants them, at the very least because they are unable to imagine them. One is alone with them, and not simply alone: one is cut off'. (Henryk Elzenberg: *The Problem of Existence*).

The poet, who often feels alone, cut off from others in his celebration of the joy of writing, still hopes that he will succeed in entering into a dialogue with at least some of the readers of his poems. He writes because he's counting on the reception of his own cognitive peregrinations. He's counting on an understanding that, even if not direct, will occur via secret spiritual bonds. One of these is the very sense of bonds common to us all, such as the fact that all of us were children once. Childhood, or more precisely, the quality of being childlike, ought to be an existential ideal for us. I reckon that our entire life is nothing more than the instinctual return of our soul to that original state of innocence, trust, delight in the world — a return to Paradise, to the freedom we once lost. Throughout a whole life of interacting with artists, returning to my favourite books, I continue to be delighted with all signs of my being bound to them, as I surrender myself to that marvellous wave of THE ONE AND ONLY, which flows through human hearts and minds. It's no coincidence, after all, that works have arisen at different times and in different places in the world which we are still able to understand and fall in love with. The authors of these works become our spiritual masters, the allies of our hearts, the friends of our thoughts, who inspire our own creativity. For me, such creative kinship has always had the greatest cognitive and existential value. Indeed, it is from this source that my poetry springs.

My first poetic masters were Julian Przyboś and Bolesław Leśmian. After them came Emily Dickinson, Rainer Maria Rilke, and Zbigniew Herbert. From Przyboś I learnt the functional husbandry of the word. Leśmian taught me to notice 'another waking life' [inna jawa] besides 'wakeful existence' [jawa istnienia]. Other poets also helped me to see into those regions of the world, in the face of which fleeting, sensory cognition stands helpless. Penetrating into the depths of things and phenomena via the word is an adventure along the lines of revelation both in the sphere of reality and in the metaphysical dimension. When I'm composing a poem, some mysterious doors open before me, which lead into a space without beginning or end. It's up to me to fill this space with my fleeting knowledge, with premonitions of heart, mind, and soul. I'm helped along this road not only by my beloved poets, but also by all the learned men and saints whom I have chosen to guide me. From long ago my device has been a message found in the *Confessions* of Saint Augustine which describes the heroism of human striving in this way: 'And so we shall seek as if we were able to find, though we shall never find anything such as will allow us to stop searching'.

The essence of poetry lies, I reckon, in this ceaselessly renewed ontological wonder: Can it be possible that amidst all the contradictions assailing me from all sides, I am fulfilled, I — the greatest contradiction, mote of dust and demiurge, in both micro and macro-scale? Can it be possible that I live and die simultaneously, at virtually the same moment? A poem does not solve contradictions; rather, it gathers them together and illustrates them as a new quality, like the eye of an imaginary lens. Writing, I am a tangle of fits and intuitions which constitute an expression that never submits to the verbalisation of striving. It is the need to send a signal, to transmit a direct communication concerning oneself, the state of one's thoughts and feelings. My intention is to initiate contact with that side of the world toward which I turn my inner sight. This might be a person, another living being, a common item, a work of art, an idea: the addressee functions as an immanent partner. The sense of the verse is to be found in the above-mentioned striving. It is undetermined and unfathomable. It bursts forth in the slivers of time between hastily noted phrases. The shape of the word, the form of the line, all ornamentation and chiselling in the workshop are secondary matters. What counts above all is that state of 'sudden eternity', of inner concentration, from which the concept of the poem is born. And it is that very immaterial value, which evades all precise definition, that stimulates me to the undertaking of ever new attempts at poeticising. In writing, I believe that I experience a sudden bedazzlement by the highest, metaphysical light. I would wish that the ray of this light should endow my writing with wings, just like the white pigeon which, thanks to the magician's sleight of hand, penetrates the prestidigitator's top-hat and transforms it too, soaringly. Such a thing would constitute a sort of proof of the intimations of childhood bearing fruit in the accomplishments of maturity.

ADRIANA SZYMAŃSKA (b. 1943) is a poet, essayist, and literary critic. She is the author of many collections of verse, two autobiographical novels, two books for children, and collections of essays. She took a degree in Polish Literature at Mikołaj Kopernik University in Toruń and moved to Warsaw in 1970, where she worked as an editor in the Czytelnik publishing house and wrote reviews and sketches for literary periodicals. To the present day, she collaborates with *New Books* [Nowe książki], *Topos,* and the *Artistic Quarterly* [Kwartalnik artystyczny]. In 2002, she moved to Pułtusk. She debuted as a poet in 1968 with a collection of poems entitled *The Heavens of Daily Life* [Nieba codzienności]. Her poems have been translated into several languages. She has taken part in many European festivals of poetry and sojourned several times in the United States as a grantee of the Kościuszko Foundation (New York), participating, among others, in the International Writing Program at Iowa City (1997). She has won several literary prizes. In 2018, she received the Fr Jan Twardowski Medal in recognition of her life work. In 2019, the PIW publishing house brought out a generous selection of her poems entitled *Uninterrupted Dialogue* [Nieprzerwany dialog], and in 2021 and 2023, respectively, the collections *Green Sunblinds* [Zielone rolety] and *Epilogue with a Star* [Epilog z Gwiazdą].

Andrzej Kotański

ELEGY ON A LEATHER JACKET

This jacket, worn by women that I've loved
And for me too it was a perfect fit,
Good Lord, when I die
When I lay this body by,
My jacket—what will become of it?

Faithful companion of my wandering,
On every nighttime crawl, and back home too ...
When I'm gone, will it to another cling,
If so, who?

It used to urge me, when the spring was nigh,
To wander through the town, hoping, and yet
Good Lord, when I die,
When I lay this body by,
My jacket—what will you do with it?

On Nowe Miasto, Plac Szembeka, chilled,
Huddling together. Days and nights when he
Warmed me — has he many left him still?
How many?

I vowed I'd never leave him. No, not I,
Not for a hundred bucks, not for a thou.
Good Lord, when I die
When I lay this body by,
What of my vow?

Andrzej Kotański   89

A SONG ON THE LIFE AND DEATH
OF FILIPPO PRINCE ODESCALCHI

A little respect! Do you want me around
To chew the cud of wealth the way you do?
I prefer newsprint over eiderdown,
It's me that pities you.

To beg spare change and vomit up cheap wine,
Hip flagon in a pocket ragged, torn,
That's what I call life. Not yours, maybe, but mine;
I can't be reformed.

Hey, you conformists, palace doll and lackey!
Frustrated in your cunning, empty, vain
Look here! See how Filippo Odescalchi
Goes down—in flame!

Two hundred forty! Hear my heart revving hot!
Straight in your face I throw your pettiness.
Get used to such new saints as these, O God!
In shallow grave beneath a bridge I'll rest.

THE POET AND THE GIRL

He brought her songs, now and then a red rose,
April was drenched with sun, and livid green.
His eyes were blue, while hers were black as sloes;
He was immortal, while she was sixteen.

What could they have in common? I don't know.
It wasn't love, because there's no such thing.
Time passed, and they passed along with its flow
As passed the days and nights with no meaning.

Soon ten years passed, and on the poet goes
With poems about spring so green and bright,
His eyes still blue, her eyes still black as sloes,
He brings a rose, but this one now is white.

Andrzej Kotański

A SAD SUNDAY

It's still not here yet, dragging its feet, the spring
the April snow lies on the naked tree
lonely through the void I go wandering
the day grey as the eyes of Anne Marie

I go from bar to bar, sit, and drink up
in silent concentration just to be
hours pass in the café each coffee cup
as warm as are the palms of Anne Marie

Dusk falls it's time to go back home Oh well
clean up the place and switch on the TV
and toss and turn where all the pillows smell
of the warm and fragrant hair of Anne Marie

THE SONG OF A MAN IN LOVE

Somewhere near the end of March, '90
traipsing lonely through Paris
in constant silent anxiety
hearing this strange song everywhere

If anything remains of me
it shall be love and I shall be
alone in every scattered part
that I'll take with me in my heart

Further and further through that grey
city I went, trying to run
from that song, which just played and played
like some grind-organ on and on

And if within my heart I keep
anything, it shall be my deep
desire alone, the deepest, sole
desire in which I'll leave my soul

And then, plodding along the Seine
I'd hum that song again and again
as if to some dictation set
so that I never should forget

Andrzej Kotański

JĘDRZEJÓW

i was born in a hospital to which
a little mortuary chapel
was attached

desk drawers
medicines letters and photos
a little flake of brown veneer
magazines paged through a hundred times
aromatic talc a perfume bottle
and sketchbooks
nothing really
nothing really except they no longer exist

i dreamt i was kneeling in the church in Jędrzejów
wiping the dust from my own gravestone
getting the knees of my white trousers dirty

and suddenly the family's no longer there
the family is dead
the mythicality of uncles and aunts
a deck of cards

—I'm cold—said granddad
—You died, we couldn't keep you in the house.
—I know but I'm still cold.

i'll call them up but what'll i say
i work i sleep i work
or maybe i sleep i work i sleep
i'm not alive mama
look me up where auntie Irka and uncle Leon are resting

i'm coming with you my dears
we'll go on a walk holding hands
toward the cemetery or toward the monastery
as worn and faded as a deck of cards
though i'm still a child
a few years old
not even twelve or thirteen

at the table with the lace doily
there's nothing but an empty seat
in this our non-existent Jędrzejów

IN THE CENTRE OF WARSAW RIGHT BEFORE AUGUST

when summer's beautiful
beautiful weather
beautiful Warsaw
especially in the city centre
where the prewar buildings still stand
on Wilcza, Hoża, and Wspólna

when i meet young people there
beautifully dressed and combed
and smiling
talking about school
about renting a flat

i know still and all
that it's nearly
august first
and they're all about to die

so much for the flat
so much
for school

VENICE—THE FINAL STROLL

Masks. Glass candies. Bright shop windows.
And an ever greater peace
Death
As an ever greater peace
Nearby music played on a piano
I'd like to die there.

Venice becomes necessary at the moment
a person becomes aware of the fact
that it's not love that's most important
but only life and death
and when in silence he greets the revelation
that death is good and beautiful
a removal of all stains
yellow pollen of goldenrod and the smell of hair
until spotless
in a faultless suit
tapping my cane against the fanning streets
i hasten my step towards one final coffee
so that the unicorn of dawn should not catch up with me

POEM WITHOUT A TITLE

One way or another we were always alone
our closest friend
our best-loved woman
were with us only to the same degree
as the snow outside the window

And all fortune telling, books, and prayers
provided only the illusion of unity
leaving us in the end
to ourselves

as if we were to begin adulthood
again and again
at every moment of existence
always crypto-infantile
looking for help and understanding
in a packet of Marlboros
in a bottle of vodka

The ivy that trembles like little bells
the poultice of hot tea upon the heart
our favourite aromas and cafés
columns, frescos, alexandrines,
all of it was nothing but a getting accustomed to
an unconditionally sober rejection
and in the end we are left alone

without a cigarette on a sleepless night

CREDO

We're here to create the myth
of ourselves
the legend of someone who donated a leaf
to inject like some malignant epidemic
the museum of our souls into the souls of those
who have no museum

We're here to live
forever — as long as we can

I believe in this earthly life
that it is
the greatest sacrum
the very heart of the mysterium
That it's today that the Resurrection plays out
the Exodus from Egypt the Fall of the Angels
upon the wet cobblestones of night

I am the cathedral.
I am the cathedral in Nevers sur Loire
the cathedral in Chartres
the cathedral in Barcelona
and again in spring
like the Ascension

and tomorrow's the first day of spring

CANTO

A man ought not to spend his life at work
That's a sin
God gave us Paris, Venice
Sezessionstil architecture, wristwatches
and Art Deco clocks
He gave us wild strawberries and
pastries with wild strawberries
hazy dawns past the café window
stores
He gave us Thomas Mann and Proust
and the bogs of Ireland too
in His wisdom He thought up
billiards and teenage girls
and a thousand other things
like waterfalls, the Divine Comedy
pipes and the poems of Rilke
streets lined with sycamores in the south
American cars from the nineteen forties
Mont Blanc fountain pens and tour guides to Granada
as well as
Cognacs and Gins, Whiskey and Bordeaux,
certainly not with this in mind
that I should be sitting
for eight hours a day
at work
like some dickhead

WINTER TEACHES LOVE

they have it best
who die at the beginning of winter

for them there's no more
digging out the car from under snowbanks
all morning long
scraping windshields and wipers
in searing cold
being stuck in traffic jams
every single day
for hours and hours

those who live must only
learn how
to love
everything that is

later
when they have
they have it as good
as the dead

for the winter no longer bothers them either

Andrzej Kotański

A TRUE STORY

when they were changing my water meter
one of the gentlemen asked
why is it so filthy here

i said that it's my brother lives here
who is mentally ill
and for that reason never cleans the place

and what's more he drinks
the plumber nodded his head
in understanding

no no
those bottles are mine
i answered

MY CONDITION IS STABLE

all right then
so it's not depression
it's a downswing of the mood
or
as you put it
despondency produced by unfulfilment
but all the same
it's atrociously stubborn and prolonged
in fact as long as I can remember
ever since I finished school
and started my first job
I've felt like this

in other words
we might say that
your condition is stable

MY PSYCHIATRIST GOES A-HUNTING

He's very proud of himself
they invited him to Yorkshire
for a gala hunt of the fox
he's even bought himself
a Harris Tweed

there'll be over a hundred people there
four dozen dogs
and then a banquet
and then a booze-up
and cetera

don't you feel sorry for the fox
I asked him

he was silent for a moment
and then he said
I feel sorry for you

IMPATIENCE

stopped at a red light
fucking red light
I say
change already

and at that moment
I hear him
in my head
speaking in that educated
wiseass deep voice of his

it's not about the light changing
it's you who've got to change

AND THIS MORNING

when I was sitting on the balcony
the Holy Spirit flew right up
in the shape of a dove
and shat on me

and what might that mean

well you know
there are some mysteries
that cannot be explained
with the aid of psychiatry

A CONVERSATION ABOUT LIFE

and so it's like this
your sex life is a failure
your professional life is too
to say nothing of your social life
failure again
is there any other life left you
to ruin

life after death

Although I studied philology for many years, I have no theory of poetry. If only I knew how to write poetry in the first place, that's what I'd do—write, not theorise. And so I thought that instead of an ars poetica, I'd talk about my most important fascinations.

The first poem that made a strong impression on me was Anna Fischerówna's 'Ballad of Jurek Bitschan'. I was five or six years old. I still hadn't spent a day in school. But I fell so strongly in love with Jurek Bitschan that I tore the page containing that ballad right out of the songbook where I found it and carried it around with me everywhere in the pocket of my little jeans . . . Of course, I lost it in the end, which only deepened the sadness I felt at Jurek's death. Soon after, I came to like Mickiewicz's 'Papa's Return'. To this day I remember the lines: '"Thank you!" sighs Papa. "Spare your breath!" / the bandit glares with angry eye. / "Long since you would have tasted death / If not for . . . Let me tell you why. / It's these your children you should thank / that thus your life I deign to spare. / For, lurking here beneath this bank, / I heard them raise their humble prayer"' There was a time when I was very fond of sung poetry: Marek Grechuta's 'Twoja postać' [Your Figure] and Leonard Cohen's 'Famous Blue Raincoat' especially.

It was in high school that I first began to reflect on why it was that I was pleased by the very things that pleased me, how they were made, and if I would be able to make something so beautiful myself. During my university years, my favourite poet was Rainer Maria Rilke. I even wrote my master's thesis about him. Beyond that, it was only individual works that made the biggest impression on me. Indeed, just such selected poems that I felt most strongly—that most powerfully resonated with my sensitivity—these held my attention the most strongly. These were authentic fascinations, becoming even objects of lengthy research. To this day, I remember the poems that delighted me so powerfully that I was moved to in-depth philological and psychological analyses. They are:

'Selma', a poem written by Vlado Dijak and later made famous by the group Bijelo Dugme. It took many years for me to understand what there was in it that moves and delights me so. It is the history of a great, unrequited love written in a very sparse, lapidary style. Well, OK, but why exactly does it fascinate me? So I set myself to a philological analysis, something that I often do when I'm not sure what to think of something—it always helps me when I write out my thoughts. And in this way, I grasped that the greatness of this poem consists in its very powerful internal conflict, the great emotional tension between the great love and the equally great incapacity felt by the lad to reveal it to his beloved. What's ravishing in it all is that nothing is literally stated concerning the greatness of the passion; rather, there is only the description of the situation. But from this, anyone can easily decipher what is playing out in the boy's soul. What is more, the form of the poem emphasises its content. What the poem does not say doubles, as it were, what the boy does not say to the girl. But beyond this, beyond its obvious aesthetic value and thrilling poetic simplicity, I understood that the most essential thing is what I felt myself, not that which tormented the hero. At this age, I myself was frequently incapacitated by shyness, unable to express my emotions. And so, I found myself in this poem, and my sympathies were directed at myself—hence the emotion that moved me.

I came to know John Keats' romantic ballad 'La belle dame sans merci' surprisingly late in life. I don't know how it could have happened that such a good poem could so mysteriously pass me by throughout my entire life, to be read by me, finally, only when I was nearing forty. All the more inexplicable was this wonder of mine at not knowing it, because when I finally did, this very verse had such an intense effect upon me. I walked about town with the poem revolving in my mind. I analysed the English original. I was persecuted by her 'wild wild eyes' and racked my brains over why there were four kisses and why it was that she went away in the first place. This is a very mysterious poem. I don't know who the girl is who was suspected of spellcasting; or who were the princes and kings from the dream, whom she had spellbound earlier. And at last, that loop in the poem, seemingly endless, emphasised by the repetition of the first lines in the last—all of this took such powerful possession of me, and my own lack of understanding so bothered me, that in the end I decided to carry out a professional psychiatric analysis along the lines of Jung's depth psychology. And I must admit that this cleared it all up for me—but I won't betray my findings here, as I've already written a separate essay concerning them entitled 'The Revenge of the Merciless Beauty' [Zemsta pięknej bezlitosnej] in the book *Niestworzone historie* [Incredible Histories].

The most tears I shed over a poem came after reading that farewell verse of Alfonsina Storni entitled 'Voy a dormir' [I'm Going to Sleep]. The most splendid thing in this poem is how the narrator is able to simultaneously reconcile a praise of life with an acceptation of her coming absence therefrom. And I, at the time, was concerned with my own personal tragedies, so this made it all the easier for me to have sympathy for the poetess who was about to commit suicide. Again and again through a sweltering weekend, I kept listening to the song 'Alfonsina y el mar' [Alfonisna and the Sea], based on this poem, becoming more and more moved with each audition. 'It's yourself you're weeping for, idiot, not Alfonsina', suddenly flashed through my head and, at the end of it all, I erupted in an explosion of cathartic laughter. Once again it so happened that the mystery was not to be found in the poem itself but, rather, in that resonating box which is the reader, in other words, me.

However, the strongest and most incomprehensible influence ever exerted on me was effected by Tomaš Venclova's untitled poem ('***') which begins with the words 'Half a mile from here, beyond the highways' knot'. Quite simply, I was reading the paper at work. Slightly bored, I was skimming through a note concerning this poet, who was completely unknown to me. I learned that he had just arrived in Poland. And then I read the poem that had been appended to the note—and I felt as if I had been struck by lightning! So strong and immediate was the sensation, like the so-called 'Sicilian lightning'—a tactile experience, for neither intellectually nor emotionally was I capable of containing it inside me. I felt a pain in my stomach and my chest cavity; I started shivering as if I had a fever and began walking in circles repeating the last strophe in an effort to somehow release the energy which had flooded upon me in such an unexpected way. I didn't understand it then, and I don't understand it still. Of course, I later came to know other poems of Venclova's available in Polish, and I came to like many of them. Still, it was always this one and only poem that had this effect on me, the same as at first. I had no port of entry into the original, as I have no competence in Lithuanian at all. And so I don't know to what extent I owe its power to the genius of its translator, Stanisław Barańczak, who was a splendid poet himself. I don't know to this day, and so I leave it. Perhaps not all mysteries must be explained.

In considering these favourite poems of mine, I noticed, of course, that the one thing that links them all together is me. If they have this special power over me, it is in me that this extraordinary sensitivity to them lies. And so the solution of their mysterious effect is not in the poems themselves, but in their receptor. A good poem awakens long-forgotten emotions, or deeply hidden secrets, in me — things that slip past my notice in my daily life. And so now I consider not just how a certain verse is formed but also what it says to me, what hideaways in my subconscious it opens when I read it. Thus, for me, poetry is a ring of keys that unlock the reader to an understanding of him or herself. By coming into contact with a good poetical text, the reader finds something in his sensitivity that generally he overlooks — at his own peril.

If I were to speak of my own composition, it is always spontaneous and unexpected. Most often it arises when I'm talking to myself. And I talk to myself almost all the time. Sometimes, in these inner dialogues of mine, there surfaces something interesting enough, or entertaining enough, that I acknowledge it worth preserving. As a consequence of this, my poems are very simple, written in an everyday, current language, the way one talks today. Sometimes we're successful in expressing ourselves in very attractive ways without even trying. That happens even quite often, but not everyone notes it down. I do. On the other hand, if one were to ask me how one goes about writing something really very good, well, I still don't know. If I knew how to write hits — Paul McCartney once joked — I'd write a lot more of them.

ANDRZEJ KOTAŃSKI, once called 'a star waiting to be discovered' by Biblioteka Kraków, is creative in poetry, prose, drama, and the sung word. He debuted in 1990 with a collection of short stories entitled *Czterdzieści siedem tysięcy bankietów* [Forty-Seven Thousand Banquets] and since then has brought out three volumes of verse: *Elegia o płaszczu skórzanym* [Elegy on a Leather Jacket, 1992], *Jutro będzie wiosna* [Tomorrow Will Be Spring, 1994] and *Wiersze o moim psychiatrze* [Poems about My Psychiatrist, 2011]. This last-named book, a bestseller in Poland, was published in English by Glagoslav of London (2022) and also adapted for the stage. Kotański is the author of a collection of short prose works, *Niestworzone historie* [Incredible Histories, 2023], one play *Wersalka* [The Couch, 2000], and has composed many original songs in Polish, as well as translating songs from Italian, Spanish, French, English, and Russian. Having studied Romance languages and literatures at the University of Warsaw (his master's thesis is a close reading of the French poetry of Rainer Maria Rilke), he has worked at the Institut Français in Warsaw and also in advertising.

Jakub Pacześniak

NEW YORK: JANUARY, EARLY FEBRUARY

Toniu in memoriam

in this city
of broken stone
it's not easy to counteract
curses

looking down
from the heights
of a hospital bed
phrases unfinished
far too much
is said of such things

the stone receives
bad news
good thoughts

retaining that
which should remain
hidden

the stone
pure in its strength
(undefiled by flesh
and blood)

teaches

the coming to know
by degrees
the complete
discovery

the maturity
to reconciliation

the hardest thing of all

Jakub Pacześniak

SEASONS

I. SPRING

a funeral cortège
heading towards the village
cemetery on a hill
already quite green
led at the front
by two flags of deep violet

II. SUMMER

by turns
rain and sun
earthworms
writhing on the asphalt

III. FALL

these dry leaves
gathered in one place
in just a moment
the wind will scatter
all over the yard

IV. WINTER

a clearing of wood
there'll be a lot of long planks
the branches already aflame
warming the woodcutters' hands

WATER

when she says
this city is inside me
I'm unable to free myself of
the erotic associations

of warm summer nights
dark ones
long remaining moist
following a July storm

of alleyways
with stillness
and the smell
of wet plaster
and rotting wood

a time in which
you still hear the dripping
the rapping of drops
the time of water
which through gutters
flows to the river
working according to its
age-old inviolable
rhythm

panta rhei? I ask
myself

this city flows
through her
and through me

through other channels
and beds
through places
that exist
inflexionally

RETURNS

To my parents

the trees of my childhood
cut down toppled
walnut pear plum
apple

the garden once
observed every day
through the window
when awoken at dawn
calmed made certain
of the stability of emotions

years later
the view transformed
raw cool

one cherry endures
broken
bearing wormy fruit

she alone remembers
she alone fears not
to shape the fruit of infirm
lips to prayers
for sun for rain
for life eternal

SUNDAY IN SEPTEMBER

the gathering of walnuts
in the tall grass
wet
from a passing shower

listening to the whispers
of the garden in fall

the cat clambering
silently
in neighbourly fashion
over the wire
so difficult to cross
fence

and so much peace
inside me

at last

THE ART OF ENDURANCE

to love in order to live
and also in order to be let down

to see the sun clearly
and the wind
to taste the stone

to be really
to go and to return

THAT'S LIFE

yes

fragile
and bindable
in hard
coffin lumber

that's faith
for those needing faith
in wind rain
and sun

such are the courses
tangled
paths
untrodden

such is silence
silence above all

and this is me
it's me calling
to you

through and through

ALWAYS WHEN DRAWING NEAR

I wound my hand
pushing back
the thorny branch
of night

I set aside old
wounds among
the wormy fruit
of the day

I strive to read
the records of stillness
in the house of your
words

I'm still here
because in me is rooted
a living seed an atom
of breath

WITHOUT COMING TO OUR SENSES

we smeared with plum jam
that best of the best
bread sliced
in gold-bearing hunks
devouring them with appetite
after which we were thirsty
standing at the threshold of a journey
planned with old
timetables for trains
which for so long now no one
sees off with their eyes
except maybe our mothers
and sisters as we wished
to see them idolators
of violets growing
on the railway embankments
stretching so far
in the direction of Zarzecze
and the forests on Babica

MY PINES

supporting the house
guardians of a pallet
of needles

branches twisted
shared meanders
of worries and joys

weighed down with snow
givers of shade
in summer

I summon you pines
spreading wide to you
the arms of the window

be my light
be a scream in the depths of me
if so needed

be the heavens bent near
or quite simply
be a wafer of tree

YOU'LL STAND LIKE THAT

at the Wisłok
or the San

just to learn that
they are rivers
real ones
as are the
sweltering days

with their great
gnarly boll
of sun

you mustn't be afraid
and I cannot
stop believing
in the shimmering
of that world
in distant voices

it's time to reforge
the ancient
language of water
into four sides
of blue

don't just stand there
go
scoop from the rivers

whole handfuls

NOTHING BUT TREE

walking I enter
amongst the trees

ever ever
closer

I touch their bark
their dry
knobbly
skin
moistened
by rain

discovering with my fingers
swellings
cracks crevasses

the desire
to lignify
the lignification of thought

to enter a tree

to feel
how they endure

so long
in one
place

I smell their leaves
I taste them

green
smooth
fresh
dry
broken

I crumble bark

peeling off the calloused
portions of epidermis
I gather branches

more slowly
more calmly

seeking a pulse
signs of life

all of these elms
maples birches
walnuts apple trees

at arm's reach
overgrow me

wind about my mind

I remain alone
I submerge myself

delving

how to get
to you

how to understand

where the road lies
to the roots
to the boughs

the branches the leaves

the road from tree
to tree?

Jakub Pacześniak

NOW YOU BRING ME

relief
if you can
stone hidden
beneath the house

shatter this my
helplessness
my irregular infirmity

insert
the living fabric
of flesh
into your perfectly
enclosed
stone circulation

live along
with the house

be

me

THE DAWN TILTS

the song of birds
toward the light

the crowns of the oaks
transparent now

somewhere there
arises the illusion
that demands
we stand still

at the foot of the hill
filled
with its litany of smells
of wood and green

the puffs of smoke flow on
voices unregistered

vanish at once

Eyes I dare not meet in dreams
                    —T. S. Eliot

WHAT FOR THIS DREAM

in which you come to learn
that you're incapable
of helping yourself to say nothing
of helping anyone you love

near and dear or distant forever
waiting counting on you
with his or her extended hand
and with eyes firmly intent on you

those hands those eyes are signs
fixed like a thorn deep in the flesh
that smoulders from the inside so
you flail about wishing to wake

beneath the widespread wings
of the hidden angel of all dreams

THE DULL ECHO

of the woodcock evoked
the soft dusk

leading nowhere
the road
good for nothing
the quiet song

but you
be merciful
to me a sinner
turn upon me
those living eyes
that never sleep

pulsing blood
sonnet of light
white stone

locked
in black
soil

Jakub Pacześniak

A CRY FROM THE SEA

Love lives not by war, its victory is life.
—Cyprian Norwid

with a plaster of bright spaces
poultice the wounded places
in the grasses waving
in the wind

let grow
the ever greater swathes
of sand
gaze about the beauty

shells stones driftwood
prayers
and day-long walks
with effort along the shore

give love
endure

as long as you can
unhurriedly

A SONG OF THE ONE ROAD

We have passed through fire and water,
and thou hast brought us out into a refreshment.
—Psalm 66 (65)

I
no one shall ever pass
the borders of a child's
innocent laughter
at life
just as no one
shall ever restrain
death

II
only at moments
of birth
and death
does time endure

III
we might look
for confirmation
in the high wind
run here
there
finding only that
which is not
of first importance

IV
every desire
ought to be nourished
so it should not die
every life
requires care

V
moving about
can be a torture
endless
exhaustion
the happiness
of the anxious

VI
one can mock
the ardour
in the fire
of glances consume
passions
see oneself not
even in a pane
of still water

VII
we move on after all
despite the pounding
of our heart
of after-images
the breathlessness
just past the threshold
having doubted a moment
let's think
what more
is needed
so as never to return

VIII
the joy of bright flowers
and the sadness of dry grass
lead one along by the same road
to ultimate
frenzy

IX
hands fingers
arms too few
to bear
the burden
of dread

X
O Lady
in thee our hope
our assistance
our
lamp on the paths
we need to pass down
pray
for us

XI
there were times we clambered up
with difficulty
racing
happily back down
feeling freedom
and the kisses
of sun of rain
on our brows and lips
there to
sprout
new thoughts
words of trust

XII
now we must
be cautious
not to reveal
over-hastily
what is hidden
to stand guard
at the last
stone of the stairs

Jakub Pacześniak

XIII
we accept and reject
what is possible
not necessarily
waiting upon all
that is most important
that is ever before us

XIV
we have not
the wisdom
the strength
which would bring
a transformation
however
we can take care
of the spirits
of travellers
stopping here
on their road
those living
meanwhile

XV
from thoughts
to deeds
the road is long
but all the same
still possible
so much
is born
on earth

XVI
we sow
the grain of goodness
evils
arrive quickly
happy he who
makes the proper
choice

XVII
that which is immobile
is transformed not
into the eternal
life is there
where everything
flows

into the wellspring

— — —

to arrive there
where end
and beginning

are given forever
and ever

ARS POETICA

I began writing before I turned twenty. Of course, that really wasn't writing with a capital W. It was more of a search, an attempt at setting my foot on the threshold of the world of literature. When does real writing begin? When you find silence in yourself. Interior silence. The poetry of silence. On the one hand, writing is the discovery of that silence, and on the other, a submerging of the self within it, within one's own, most important, silence. Perhaps in order to be able to come to recognise both your strengths and your weaknesses. And both of them enjoy equal rights. You work as an apprentice in the school of humility. The more texts you toss away, the better it is for you as an author. Because you must approach the word slowly. The word stands on guard at the entrance to the house of poetry. It's at the start; it's the entrance point, but it's also the goal, the finish line, the end, the limit. The word is a vessel capable of bearing (almost) everything. The construction of such a house can be a way to bestow sense upon your life. Especially when that house is filled with love, people, God or gods, trees, stones, all the good, and maybe even dangerous animals with whom you'll need to struggle . . . and when through the middle of it there flows a river of crystal-clear water.

I do not like the poetry of screams, of revolutionary slogans. In my case, writing was never rebellion. Rather, it was a completion, a continuous attempt at the completion of myself and the world that was given me to contemplate. I've always been fascinated with contemplative poetry. Unhurried poetry, even confessional poetry — but the latter only to a certain degree. For a person ought to keep certain things to himself. It's not right to speak of everything aloud, nor can you express everything aloud. You can signal many things, make use of poetic figures of speech, a word . . . and allow the reader to do the rest, filling in the blanks. I am an enthusiast of terse poetic statement, in the creation of which the receptor also plays a role in the evocation of sense. As a reader, the poetry that made the most profound impression on me was, of course, first of all that written by the authors of my homeland with which I came into contact at different times in my life, and it was not always poetry of the short form. Among my masters I would name Różewicz, Herbert, Grochowiak, but also Baczyński and Gajcy, Czechowicz, and most certainly Norwid. As far as our Nobel winners are concerned, I'm closest to Miłosz, especially Miłosz of his later period. Also important to me as poets are Julian Przyboś, Stanisław Piętak, Wiesław Kulikowski and Stanisława Kopiec. Sons and daughter of the same land—the Subcarpathian land—in which I matured, from which I travelled on to study Polish and Czech literature at university. Thanks to the latter, I drew close, in turn, to the poetry of Vladimír Holan, Jan Skácel, Bohuslav Reynek, and Ivan Blatný. I also learned a lot from English-language poets: E. E. Cummings, John Berryman, William Carlos Williams, Dylan Thomas, and especially T. S. Eliot, of whose poetry I comprehended little at the start, but then slowly and more surely, I ventured into that world of his thanks to my father, who was a great lover of the poetic paths of the author of *The Waste Land* and, in turn, my guide along them.

I have always admired and been fascinated by double entendres and equivocal arrangements of words. Toying with sense. I've always enjoyed submerging myself in such poems, racking my brain and trying, as well as I might, to write in a similar way—at least for a certain time, as there are not that many poems of that type in my work. Still and all, I hope that those which yet exist have a certain value. My first and second volumes end with such poems, which might be understood in different ways according to their graphic arrangement. The first of these is 'and perhaps for example the word'. It is made up of just three lines:

a może poeta jest mordercą
rozcina na przykład duszę
i wywleka wnętrzności słowa

[and perhaps the poet is a murderer
who slits open for example the soul
disembowelling the innards of the word]

It can be read as it is written, and understood. But one can also eliminate from its contents the words which are in the title. In that way, a new verse appears, and the sense is changed: 'the poet is a murderer / who slits open the soul

/ disembowelling the innards'. The poem that brings my second volume to a close is also multisignificative. It possesses several meanings which can be obtained by inserting a pause in different places. Why? Because language is too rich for us not to take advantage of its largesse.

a teraz zamknij mnie
w ciemności słowa
zamieniają się miejscami*

And one more thing. The poetry of the province. Of my world. Regions where nature is close at hand, from which the chaos of the city is absent, have a gigantic, if not fundamental, significance for me. I'm a different person in such places. The great majority of my poems arise in the province, in my native Boguchwała, to which I constantly return, at the Baltic Sea coast, in the mountains, or in a village near Kraków. Quite simply, there, where I experience peace. Silence. That inner silence. I don't want to suggest that I'm unhappy in the city. Kraków, where I've spent the majority of my life, Budapest, or Prague, in both of which I spent several years, all have their charms, but that is where I earn my daily bread; that is where I fulfil my duties. There I have less time for reading, less time for writing. The province has its own charm which speaks to me, also through the poetry of such authors as Bolesław Leśmian or Tadeusz Nowak. When I grow old, I plan to move somewhere far away from civilisation. Let that be my 'age of gold'. Enchanted by nature, in the midst of forests, streams, on dusty roads and trackless wastes, barefoot . . .

---

* *Translator's note*: Because of the inflected nature of the Polish language, in which the word *słowa* at the conclusion of line two may be either a genitive singular or a nominative plural, the word-play mentioned by the author is perhaps impossible to recreate in a noninflected language such as English, where unambiguous choices of prepositions must be made. There are at least two ways of reading this poem in Polish, both natural: 1) 'And now enclose me in the darkness, the words exchange places'; 2) 'And now enclose me in the darkness of the word / they exchange places' (the subject of the verb — they — being undefined, unless *ciemności* is a plural [i.e. 'darknesses'], which it can be).

JAKUB PACZEŚNIAK is a poet, translator, and scholar of Polish and Czech literature. In 2000, he published a poetic leaflet *Ich pięć* [The Five of Them] as well as collections of poetry: *Własny rachunek* [One's Own Account, 2001], *w ciemności słowa* [In the Darkness of the Word, 2011] and *dno oka* [The Depth of the Eye, 2019]. From the Czech he has translated, among others, the prose of Bohumil Hrabal, as well as librettos and poetic cycles to the music of Antonín Dvořák and Leoš Janáček commissioned by the National Opera of Poland. His own poetry inspired the musicians of the Buen Camino group from his hometown of Boguchwała to create the album *Powroty. Drzewa mojego dzieciństwa* [Returns. The Trees of My Childhood, 2003]. His work has been translated into many languages, including Czech, Slovak, and Hungarian. He has taught Polish literature at universities in Olomouc, Budapest, and Banská Bystrica. Recently, along with Stanisław Dłuski, he edited the *Flisz poetycki. Antologia najazdu awangardy na Rzeszów* [Poetic Flysch. An Anthology of the Avant-Garde Invasion of Rzeszów, 2022]. He is the *spiritus movens* behind the Siemaszkowa Literary Festival *Międzysłów Karpat*. Former director of the track and field section of the AZS AWF Sports Club in Kraków, he continues to referee the sport. Currently, he is employed at the Book Institute in Kraków, near which city he lives. His newest collection, *plaster jasnej przestrzeni* [a plaster of bright spaces] was published in 2025.

Artur Grabowski

HE HESITATES

The ocean's even breath. With certainty, monotony
the wave sows trash and takes it back at once. The adoration
unceasing of the ritual free will that moves the line
there on the sand. Pebbles eternal, abandoned shells,
the supple bodies from the epoch of the first kingdom.

After a week (sometimes even earlier) I grow bored
with this game of give-and-take, which cheaply mirrors life.
But on the first day (usually toward evening): the weak certainty
that it's all a pendulum motion — even
footsteps forward.

Memory takes on a pathetic rosy hue in the west.
I allow myself to believe in the rhythm of sacrifice and reward.
The momentary crack between escape and second coming:
horizon, horizon — necessary delusions.

Figures descend from the canvas and the dazzled sun-
    bathers uncover
the background; fabric checkerboard from beneath the
    darkening colours.
Somewhere a star will flash, as if winking
from the other shore.

   He stares his way into speechlessness. The ocean
   poses no questions now, but his breath responds:
   even, and calm, unchanging, at one
   with truth.

August, 1998

POMPEII (NOTES FOR A POEM)

What disastered a city [...] is visually patent.
    —W. H. Auden

1.

The city, which did not survive
only so as to endure.

A punishment for market calculations?
or flaws liturgical in rituals?
Or perhaps a gift for fat retirees
dressed down for heat in shorts and baseball caps?

2.

Time, like a flame, darts its tongue
between the mud of streets and the dust-covered
archeological terrain, between
the rough wall of the temple and the slippery
entrails of the sacrificial bull. Tamed

the fire lived alongside them — even here
there was winter — someone warmed his hands
and someone else gave into the seduction
of light between the wood and the ash.

3.

The imagination completes the colonnade
(order — a pagan grace of resurrection?)
and exhaustion finds at last a hard bench
(the body — is it that, indeed, which dies not?)

And where have those two thousand eighteen years gone?
Not even a powdery sense remains
which one needs to rinse off one's skin
upon return to the hotel. Just like then...

there will be meat and red wine for supper,
and we go to the cubiculum, and later
fall asleep.

We'll only dream our own
films, though within the limits of probability.
Something repeats and the recollection
gives us pleasure. 'Cos what can you expect
from people?

4.

The sun dries the bottles
in the post-imperial alleyways,
in villas, in temples, in public
baths and in houses of peaceful love.

There is no water. Only sweat and a dry
tongue remember it and desire
its return. Water, we ache for you
as for money! And bottles?
Ah, they endure; today
they interest us not.

The forms in which we captured satisfaction
(that cool in the shadow of the great vase)
will wait us out alongside
our bodies.

5.

And everybody's pointing at the ruts
cut by a slow cart—laden with wine barrels?—
into which the swift chariot plunged

Two parallel stream beds
(in rainy weather),
two corridors, canyons, ditches
tectonic. Thanks to them
the Roman citizen was free
from doubt. The two-wheeled

single-track, or velocipede, is the invention
of liberals, like the Harley or Honda
minibike—against the grain.

To drag the metaphor out, one might say
its stability was guaranteed by continual

pursuit or escape . . . But realms
lasting millennia must promote
war as well as commerce, careful
to preserve some balance.

6.

The guides compare: Here they sold wine,
and here, please, have a look at these sketches, legionnaires
made these things. Nothing's changed? Ho-hum:

we still drink from cups, and pictures reveal
likenesses. Questions of finishing touches? Sure, only that
we touch is ephemeral. There where the senses can't
reach, one can always make deductions,
somewhat riskily.

From the lack of evidence we place our trust
in traces and testimonies. For otherwise
what would there be for us to love but bare
walls, without hope of reciprocity?

7.

Grass in the cracked mosaic,
a layer of sand right at the bottom of the pool,
dwarfed trees and herds of pebbles
that push themselves into one's shoes.

If it was nature — the senses
might somehow submit to bewilderment, but
we're pinched by what is endless.

Is that why they've survived
those frescos, those sublime statues
so that we'd value significance
more than life? For whom

did he decorate walls and floors, whom
did he hate, scratching walls
with graffiti? What did he see
in the flat face in the fountain?
If it exists — it exists
for me.

8.

The way it looks is, if not for the volcano,
nothing would have been preserved. It'd all have fal-
-len to pieces, memory, like papyrus unhidden
in time before the epochal flames.

The earth is waiting like a narrative
poem covered in the dust of overinterpretation.

All we can be sure of
concerning this is the
explosion. And then began archeo-
-logy, in other words the exhumation of white
fragmenta antica from beneath the hard-packed soil.

Our notes, cards, scrawling
will be your little garden, plot, at most
unconsecrated host.

9.

The ruins remain. Although they wished
to leave us fulness — we've chosen life.

Ah well, cheer up
we have something to latch on to
— some contact, at least.

Hold to the edge
of the last line — two boards
nailed together with living flesh:

goodness is timeless.

THE GREY MAN

In the black and white film on Alberto Giacometti the sculptor
(skinny, thick sports-coat and scarf) sits
before the figure (ell-tall) resting upon a high
chair; the grey figure stands with its back
to us, sex and face on the other side,
you can clearly see the branches
of its limbs and the stick of its spine.

    the head has become an object
    without dimensions

The artist looks like a potter
who instead of smoothing the hips
of the spinning vase, with quick movements
kneads and pinches, correcting
and risking; but the changes
are small, too precise
for the eye to register;
he's smoking a cigarette too, sometimes
he glances at the camera through the smoke
a moment later he begins to wrap
the clay with a damp cloth
and leaves it like that, till next time.

    large figures were for me
    false, and small ones —unbearable

At last he rises; the finished sculpture
enters the frozen frame and waits;
the hard shadow of the skeleton might
bear flesh of ash and spittle;
in the background (fuzzy) appears a back
bent beneath the heavy beam of shoulders,
AG exits through the wall
of his Paris studio
and then sits down on the stoop
of his family home in the Alps.

If I knew how to draw them
There'd be no need of creating
them in space

And now we are
one on one: in front of me,
at the height of my own head,
the little, heavy, grey
man; naked, bent
like someone who takes a decisive
step forward, bearing
exactly so much as not to fall
beneath his own weight:
an old man's texture, a boy's shape, the size of a newborn.

in reality none of these objects, only
all at once

GOOD-BYE

It's late October. Before the rainy times
The beeches store their warmth, the maples breathe
Gold light. Hushed feet brush through leaves crushing rime.

I feel the chitin slumber of the soil break
Beneath my tread; the slick sucks the white mist that
Shatters the air. Careful, with each step I take

I sculpt will into dread: Not in this divot
Must it remain, this valley, ever nearer,
Form-fitting. Disgust. Yes, that is the pivot

Of the potter's wheel. Immortal clay, that grows
Unto the skies, on the wind's palm. Water jug,
Sand and birches. Like bones impaled. There is no

Frost yet to seal with marble plate the fields of fall.
Warm afternoons reek of naphtha: collar lining
Fawns the neck with plastic fur. No, no one calls

Me from my home or mountain or the river.
Well, decide. Now, will you love the yellow mob
Of young lindens, or that snarl of sticks, withered

In August at the garage wall, wild grape vine.
The pigeons remain. But are they brave? Yes?
Courage and determination in a grime

Of exhaust fumes? The lanterns still glow. In vain.
And yet. Their rosy bellies—trusting, urgent, stupid—
Like a dog's barking. Heavy and flaccid, plain

Before me, a vision: crushed cans, cards, thrown
Away, split edges, flaked shavings, scratched and gnawed
Scurf . . . Rubbish tumbled. He draws near me, my own

Afterliver. Ashtrayed (at home) the fags die
To ash. The glow draws in the dry. And the red
Womb of the world withdraws. It's dark now. Good-bye.

TRIPTYCH (PART I, LEFT)

At morning (not 'at daybreak') when they're still
sleeping in the tent, I go out
onto the narrow path
above the glassy mirror of the lake;
the freshly cut timber
smells like wet flesh; I hop
on the springy planks, my steps
knocking at the void over ever deeper water.

I arrive at the end, turn around, sit down:
the wooden road (tracks without rails) driven
into the beach at a gap in the high shore;
behind me (a little recollection, a little imagination) the sky
in a greenish mirror, the wall of the woods.

The strips of mist like a flock of sheep
pasture above the waters
on either side of the bridge,

of which I am (time to go back) a pillar.

Artur Grabowski   153

TRIPTYCH (PART II, RIGHT)

Between the clouds the sun strikes, pinching the skin
towards storm; a pale shadow circles
tight around me, every step from an unexpected
side; warmth, the soft smell of the grass, but
I'm alert. I observe

her reptile dartings: she runs
to the very edge of the pier, suddenly stilled like
a photograph; and again to the beach, to the white ring
tangled in green vines, there she grows still
gazing at the boat facing the opposite
shore; she stands there long until unexpectedly once more

lurching off, to stand again in the middle, kneel
and carefully (carefully!) arrange herself on the edge
(I feel her cheek cuddling against the fragrant
mama pine), she stretches her hand, can't reach,
leans near again (to run up?) until at last
she touches. I make myself visible, wave from afar, at last
I enter her gangway like a corridor at home;
I lay down beside her, she allows me to stare:

between the flashing water and the misty sky,
with finger-tips, she smears the reflected image.

TRIPTYCH (PART III, CENTRE)

At the end of the long footbridge
a blue man in a red cap
sits staring at a coppergold
splotch on the water; his long stick, thin
as a crack, points to the orange wheel
pinned on the horizon.

You can't see the line but for sure
it links him with the innards of the lake.

Behind him his thin shadow
printed on the planks,
before him, dwarfed, his reflection:
the shaky film of an amateur.

From the shore all three persons can be clearly seen.

    I know for sure that soon they'll
    disappear: first the sharp contours,
    then the illusive similarity
    and at last the heavy presence.

    It's then I cry: Grandpa!
    Grandpa! Grandpa!
    and here he comes.

EMANATION

In the window frame: the mask's white shade
moving at the pleasure of my head;

or the sky: ever farther, ever brighter,

with the dimly stamped woodcut:
the skeleton of an apple-tree gone wild.

A flat box? What it
sucks in it penetrates;
an old icon, a late forgery.

***

Tiny voids glowing hot
in the charred heavens
gaze down at me
as if I were
a mirror.

SLEEPING WITH PERSEPHONE

Shutting off the light you say: *The eyes*
grow accustomed to the darkness. Your tanned body
emanates a pale glow like a cloud of breath in freezing weather;
the cracked triangle on your behind, still brighter, emboldens
hope for an exit, two white breasts gazing at the wall
behind me. *At night*—you say—*The shadows of the Earth*
   light up
our inner selves, the words are on our side.

ETERNAL REST

I read your message: unimportant
news: something about what I need
to buy for supper. One ordinary service
among so many we render life. Later I returned
to reading the poems of a foreign poetess. Suddenly

I remembered that for God's sake I got
a message, so I reached for my phone, but then
I remembered that that, which is now
has already been. So I returned to reading
poems and remained with them until the next morning.

    I guess I must have fallen asleep, because I don't
        remember if I finished
here or there. I felt so rested as if I'd done
something completely unimportant. Something that
        doesn't demand the least
effort. Or courage even. Or memory even. Or waiting even,
without which how I'd rush to you over that river
of foreign bustle. Or even words, for the lack thereof,
        for God's sake,
we'd be hungry all night long.

Artur Grabowski

SCRAPING AND STIPPLING

Scaly skin, frosted window frames and fluffy
fields — afar, afar. From buttock to back
and neck the shiver slides fetched by fingers;

as if I really could read and write a tongue
soundless. Where shall it lead me this ignorance
of eyes? These wildly swelling tropes — articulation

to impression? At each stop I touch the next
ring. But rather than descending I emerge
onto platforms abandoned by idlers. Wagons

stretch out tactile points in the space between
departure and the last moment before return
home. We have so much to add that we free-fall

into each other like two blurring haphazard frames
of abstract photography. The depths set
breath on the surface, which at the contact

answers the blind man's questions.

EXODUS

We tore the cobweb, hindered by no one.
A group of emigrants, a group of immigrants.
The forest is both asylum and trap, no?
A little less at home than trees and mushrooms,
like a stream searching out its bed, we meander.
Our traces ornaments for birds —you reckon?
Before the rains wash them away, we'll be
ever closer, ever closer to our
soaked shirts, in an eiderdown sewn
of our sweat and the needles of foreign pines
clinging to fear and illusive clearings,
we'll find the field with logs like benches, weave
our lean-to there and light the bonfire. Tell
me a story. There will be no night, only dreams.

COLLABORATORS

This happened long ago. Before the war and before the
    pestilence,
Before the great hunger and petty apocalypse. Bent low

Before the ranks of corn cobs in their little green uniforms,
We cleared the fields of weeds . . . My arms ached as did my
    back,

But I slashed furiously with my mattock at the stiff hard stalks,
Caring not that the root of the harmful plant might
    remain whole

Untouched in the earth. The late afternoon field was full
Of the emaciated, bitter-smelling, bronze-skinned fallen.

Exhausted and filthy we rode later proud and lordly
On a tractor to the supermarket for beer. Vacations

Spent in the Rheinland or Hesse (black market work)
Got us the funds we needed for Greece, Italy, Provence.
    After all

Our Bauer (an accountant by trade) was not stupid. Why
Did he tolerate our sloppy work, looking away and
    rewarding our piecework?

And us? Had we forgotten that next year again the jungle
Would invade the croplands? I'd like to believe we
    thought of future

Generations of slaves who, just like us, would break free
    of the boredom
Of universities and come here in the summer to do
    gymnastics for pay. But

That's not true. The German knew us well. He knew that
    we know
That these things pass not away: war, hunger, plague, little
    catastrophes and the desire

For beauty.

WE'RE PASSING THROUGH

Flat lands. Termite hills, sometimes something that's no longer
tree, nor yet a bush. Neither lake
nor river dare be expected lest you risk
mockery. Logic works perfectly here, and experience
unconditionally. The desert must be deserted (Right?) that
    means,
with little exceptions to prove the rule
in premises. We ride on squeezed together ten of us
in a car made for five. Because that's what fate
wanted, alias profit (once fortune, then lottery) and the greed
of the free man? Sand sifts sand. The straightaway
splits windscreen like a spike. It's getting ever narrower
and yet nothing changes. Flat lands. Termite
hills like phalluses or chopped oak saplings. Poetry
allows metaphorical freedom (Right?) in the bounds
of a province enclosed by dialect. Long way yet to
town. Where each of us has something
before him.

Kenya, Turkana, December 2023

MEDITERRANEAN LANDSCAPE

It's really dark. Although it's unbelievable, the black
fingers of a palmtree leave their prints on the black
    quarter of the night captured
in the frame of the window and crucified: one arm has
    fallen from the beam
to hang somewhere at the height of the nail piercing the feet,
the other supports (but only on the drawing) the head
    surrounded with the wire
of stiffened hair. Sight immobilised registers the tiny
steps of time in the rhythm of barely distinguishable
    quavers. The cool
wind cannot penetrate the pane but the sweat on the skin gels
into a tight armour of frost. I'd rather not get up, but
    here I am standing
in the depths of an interior remembered — alone on the
    threshold between
house and garden.

(FROM THE CYCLE 'THREE ISLANDS')

The little Russian girl found a hedgehog
and now wants it to give her a sign
of life. The hedgehog stubbornly feigns
death. It really takes talent
not to move an inch yet be
somewhere else. At last, however
nothing interesting for a child. Nadia
(I heard her Daddy call her) carries
the little animal into the bushes by the wall
where she found it, and returns
with a sad expression, empty hands
to her people. And over there in the wings
the little hedgehog shrugs off the costume
and stands naked before the cicadas' orchestra;
the tutti of the violin drowns out his
newborn wail. I can't hear
that, obviously, because only
what's obvious penetrates
to me through the night.

2020

Artur Grabowski

(FROM THE CYCLE 'THREE ISLANDS')

I remember dreaming about
a butterfly. Later I saw
it on the cliff. I stood at the edge: down below
two women were walking along the shore, the sea
was kissing their feet, the flame of their ruddy hair
did battle with the wind. Suddenly they halted and looked
upward. I wanted to say something to them, but
I was afraid that my words might pull
me down after them. The butterfly circled
around my head above the waves and above
the meadow. They must have been sirens
because on the sand I found
no footsteps. The wind was at my back and I was
the mast of an island drifting —
the fragile and only
axis of the
h o r i z o n

2020

(FROM THE CYCLE 'THREE ISLANDS')

We're erring over trackless wastes. The labyrinth of freedom
mocks us with its red palate full of little granite shoots,
striving to pierce our tires with the ferocity of an old man
gone infantile. For two wild asses this does not exist this
    caricature
of life, which whines and belches gasses, but never goes
    into heat
to be mounted. Yes, we're dead, so we can look on
as the dust sticks on the window of our curiosity. Thoughts
bored through by the little insects of the alphabet will
    travel through the desert
and the sea of doubt will part before them. The road
at last grips the underbelly, to give us progeny
in an unlooked-for village. We sit down to a wedding
feast, wine is spilt like blood on a battlefield. The sun
sinks into the earth, the bodies of nameless sheep unite
    with the bodies
of our caresses. People talk and sing in the language
of wolves and shepherds. We get it: it's all
over.

2020

Artur Grabowski   167

(FROM THE CYCLE 'THREE ISLANDS')

Once these olive groves — I reckon — gathered the light
of lamps; by it someone licked words from letters, and
    someone else's
lips set bronze on the skin of someone's shoulders, or
    pressed the cherries
upon the faces of two breasts. Today we can only sense
the taste of that predestination. God arrives rarely, ravishing
with a quick rainfall, so hundred year old bellies and
    arms tempt
him with their unending dance and cracked skin.
    The matte bodies
of ancient lizards migrate over them suddenly from death
to death, petrified in brief meditations on the first
dragon, who decayed into a million Doppelgängers so as
    to endure
in an age of miniaturisation. The blade of the horizon
    scrapes the relief
from the disk of the sun, the wound glows like the flesh
    of an orange. I shut off
the engine and roll down the window. In the darkening
    spaces between trees
a chorus of inhuman spirits encased in chitin armour
strikes a spark. I wait until anxiety shall say: Go.

2020

CERTAINTY AND MYSTERY

A poet, even if he makes his living as a professor of poetry, feels a reluctance to speak of his own poetry. But ... called up to the blackboard by Prof. Kraszewski, I couldn't refuse him, not Karol, for one doesn't refuse one's friends, even if one is by nature a recalcitrant student. So what's to be done, except scrawl a few sketches ...

It will be a complex figure in the end, which I'm sketching as one ideogram. For one it might be like a sand drawing, a mandala; for others, a stained-glass window. But even if you see in it nothing but a pattern for a carpet, that'll be all right too; enjoy, may it be soft to your feet.

I believe in poetry, and I believe poetry, and I believe through poetry.

I believe that, despite what Auden says, it is through poetry that all that can happen in the human world does happen. Because everything that happens in the human world happens as understanding. Understanding expressed is a confession of faith in the real.

The poem opens to the light that falls upon the tongue. Through the tongue, the consciousness casts light upon the experienced object sunk in gloom, the object that is, what is. If right now the image that occurs to you is the cosmic order: Sun–Moon–Earth, well, you've caught a glimpse of poetry.

Poetry, that cosmic order, unfolds itself in words by degrees, because it wishes to reveal itself to people. Language is the human form of existence. Expression is always the revelation of some manner of being. One can search for poetry in the stars or in the heart, but one always remains in the cosmos.

The content of the poem is the emotional-intellectual state of existence. The poem expresses nothing; it transforms a manner of perception. Having found oneself in this distinct state, we believe wholeheartedly, for a moment, that things are, that they happen, just so.

This certainty has the power of conviction. And convictions push towards incarnation in words, pushing, at the same time, the limits of the ongoing experience of life. Through the poem, that which we call 'life' or 'world' appears to us as experience incarnate in words — an experience which is by some miracle both intimate and universal.

Revelation? To suggest something like that would reveal a lack of humility. So perhaps: the absurd? That, on the other hand, would be arrogance. Certainly, a type of a risk, because it always reveals its source, which is trust. And so are we talking about thought? Yes, thought, but thought before all rationalisation. Not: thoughtlessness, but: prereflection incarnate in words.

Have you noticed that in saying 'reflection', I'm summoning the moon once more for aid? Begging nothing of the sun except grace.

And so — thought, and so — speech, and so — writing. Each of these in its own way arrives in the world from beneath the heart, beneath the stars. Can it be that this has something in common with the act of birth? An annunciation, anxiety, joy. Well, that's how it happens.

The Greeks had a special word for this: *poiein*. That means neither creation, nor construction, nor composition — but, rather, the spinning of something essentially new, which at the same time does not lose its kinship to its source. The words *semiosis* and *ecstasis* describe similar processes. The first signifies the inception of meaning, the transformation of objects into signs, while the second refers to the process of shaping the unique and unrepeatable, surprisingly overt form out of the gloomy and shapeless reality that precedes it.

Poetic thinking spins itself out of itself, weaving a web in which flies buzzing nearby are trapped. When a fly blunders into a spider's web, the web trembles. And it is then that we hear that the web is a stringed instrument.

In writing a poem, I set free the instrument that plays its own composition.

Poetry surprises me in myself and demands of me that I become a poet—for a certain time. At such a moment I try to be as passive as possible. My activity is based on an alternating current of attention: an active opening—and a passive closing—of lips.

Breathing? Singing? Isn't that what our body's for?

The writing of a poem is a manner of listening to reality. Writing a poem, I try, quite simply, to sing its score, which slowly emerges in the process.

I eavesdrop on the rhythm that the poem draws out of me. The rhythm of the poem babbles in me like a stream over rocks and trembles like a spider's web under the weight of a fly.

The poem teaches me its rhythm until I learn to express what I can't hear until I express it. In saying 'rhythm', it's not sounds that I have in mind. The rhythm of a poem is a symptom of the order of meanings which reveal themselves in words when the same assume the character of poetic expression.

But where does this poetic nature of words come from? Is poetry an inexhaustible collection of verse? And the work of the poet anamnesis? Does poetry simply wait for someone to make room for it? And, what does that mean: make room? For example, to lie down on a broad meadow ... and look up at the stars from there, listen to the pulse of the body from there.

If right now a lazy shepherd has occurred to you, I won't say that I'm not trying to imitate him.

Poetry becomes present in time. The poet draws from poetry, which has revealed itself to him in its current form. He needn't know this, just as an athlete doesn't need to know anything about anatomy and physiology. It's his body that knows.

Poetic tradition is a long process of limbering the tongue, the result of which is an ever-greater sensitising of our ability to verbalise the experience of reality.

The Greeks are the forefathers of us poets, and it was they who held that the first poet was a shepherd. A caretaker of animals destined for the slaughter?

I get the sense that this model imposes a certain obligation upon me, that it sets before me a challenge which is not so easy a one, morally speaking. It is for this reason that it so happens that the writing of a poem gives rise, in me, to dread. Here comes an expression which in and of itself aspires to express reality, at the same time making someone responsible for it, someone who is not entirely its author.

You might sense in this a hedging of bets, or modesty, but I reckon that, in a certain sense, every poem is authored by all poets, past and future.

Poetic speech is not necessary to man — not for him to secure the conditions of continued existence — but it is necessary for him in order to exist humanely amongst other human beings. For this reason, poetry will last as long as human speech will last.

Poetry is not eternal, but it is long-lived. It is preceded by silent understanding, which existed amongst people before the emergence of speech and which shall return, when we come to understand everything.

When I'm writing a poem, I'm not doing it of myself, for myself, or on behalf of myself. I'm receiving a guest, and even so, not as a host at his own hearth, but as the hearth itself. The life experience of the poet is the poem's home; the poem will take possession of that home so as to invite wanderers inside.

If you now picture a naive and sentimental sketch of a country forecourt or some wayside inn, perhaps you've already arrived at the end-point of this essay-map that I'm aiming for.

A poem convinces us not so much by the perfection of its wording as by our sense of the importance of what it says. Poetry won't allow me to doubt that what I indubitably experience wants to be significant for me.

Both the experience and the significance belong to the human area of existence. If the poem contains both of these in itself, the poem must be someone rather than something. It's no coincidence that we speak of the lyrical 'subject'.

The poem has an autonomous existence, but—just like a person—it will not be itself without needing someone. The poem will be someone if it will be somebody's.

Independent of grammatical regulations, each poem is written in the second person—to you.

The essence of language is poetic—language signifies, because it marks an experience which, thanks to this fact, delivers itself up to a person's reading. The reading experience—the deciphering of that which is—this is the fundamental task that allows a person to exist in a human manner.

When the reader begins to sing aloud what he's carefully deciphered, embracing with attention the signs of his own experience, then poetry becomes present amongst people.

The poem allows me to sing as if I were playing on the instrument of my own voice, so that other people hear, not me, but the music of the poetry.

The spider sings by the trembling of his web, and his entire body listens to this composition. You've got to dance out this image, grasping it with your ear.

The sung reading of characters by which language marks our experiences is the incessant adoration of the world presented to attentive human perception. We adore that which is impossible to ignore. Adoration is belief, mental belief as well, made incarnate in human action.

Finish the sentence yourself: I believe..., I think..., I love... The act of expressing in words cannot be separated from the content of what is being expressed.

And what is it that you see now? A shaman, confident of his powers, or a bashful, disconcerted lover?

It's no coincidence that every great religious tradition expresses itself in figurative language: in images evoked by words, in metaphors, in parables. But even poetic texts that contain no religious content are a solidified confession of faith in that which cannot be negated. What is more, faith needn't correspond to trust; it can also be a confession of distrust that leads to faith in the opposite of what is real.

We might make a poetical confession—I might even say we can't do otherwise—of faith in reality deprived of religiously understood transcendence. There's no way of resisting the sensation of the poems of Paul Celan, providing testimony to an encounter with a personalised Nobody, whereas the poems of Wallace Stevens are a confession of faith in an impersonal Something. Dante Alighieri's great epic is a description of a world which cannot be anything but the work of a transcendent Creator. But Lucretius' epic describes a world that demands some human creator to make use of it as matter for his own creation.

By what miracle do each of these works seem equally convincing?

The poem adds nothing to reality; it configures the experience of the same. It pushes the borders that we have grown accustomed to set about the comprehended world.

Restraining the rational practices of Reason or pushing Reason beyond the limitations of the activity proper thereto, Poetry wins an authority over reasoning, wresting from Reason the right to any autocratic decision of what is, or is not, understandable.

I don't mean to say thereby that poetry is necessarily incomprehensible by reason. I wish to say, rather, that reason ceases to serve comprehension whenever it abandons poetic expression, which, after all, it makes use of inexorably. Such reason reasons not. It merely plays at ratiocination.

Please, fear not—neither the algorithms of artificial intelligence, nor the mechanisms of behavioural psychology, nor the physiological processes of the brain will ever take the place of human thought. Only by thinking poetically can man make use of reason in a human manner.

Plato feared poetry because he reckoned, and rightly so, that it enslaves thought. And yet he himself thought in this way, surrendering himself to poetry like a lover blinded by love. Does poetry, then, blind a person? Well, after all, Homer, the prototype of all poets, is supposed to have been blind. Can such a blinding of the mind and senses result in comprehension?

The poem blinds because it dazzles with light. It wants to enlighten the mind with light reflected from things and transmitted through the body, which exalts human liberty. Does poetry lead us out of the cavern? Can this metaphor of Plato's not reconcile those two rivals, Dante and Lucretius?

The moment when poetry strikes the mind certainly unfolds to mystery. Certainty and mystery cannot be divided. They are like two sides of one coin; they are, like clasped hands, a reciprocal being.

Ezra Pound compared the word to a coin, Czesław Miłosz to a handshake, and both of them had in mind communication by means of symbol, in other words, object or significant gesture. The coin is no mere glittering piece of metal, and the handshake is not just contact with someone else's body. We make use of coins and handshakes because they possess value.

We can exchange a coin for something; we can buy something that we wish to offer to someone else. Things encompassed by reasoning, in other words, the whole conglomeration that we call the world, belong to no one, but they're not just common property. They are in constant circulation amongst us. When we offer someone our hand, we engage in an exchange of presences, we visit one another reciprocally in our homes. The place which I inhabit on account of my reasoning is always, also, the place where others come to be (even in loneliness) and the place in which I am someone else's guest.

The poetic use of words establishes the human community, in contrast to practical speech, which merely regulates inter-personal relations.

In contradistinction to science and philosophy, which ought to speak of things with humility, poetry permits itself to express something in words unapologetically.

The poem constantly fills itself with the content of human understanding, which it comprehends in itself, while not sealing it off exclusively. It's like a vessel of permeable membrane. For this reason, the poem lasts as a source of understanding, a source which is actually never exhausted, although the intensity of its active nature can be alternating, can even cease revealing itself to people as a source. At such a time in place of the poem, we note a waste land, which promises nothing to no one.

Can you see the map now? Beautiful, isn't it? Nothing is hidden behind it; it reveals everything that surrounds us. By reading a map, the mind takes one, physically, on a journey through space.

Nothing happens without the participation of poetry, because we are unable to take any decision which would not be preceded by an agreement or an opposition to something that has sense, significance, importance.

It's no coincidence that these three words are, basically, synonyms. As if they were indicating the same thing from different sides. As if through our particular, freely made choices in reference to them, we were adoring the object of our faith. As if we possessed the certainty that that which is, is evinced as a mystery and therefore demands comprehension by the reason, the result of which will be a decision, not mere knowledge.

By allowing us to use words familiar to us from of old in a manner which we did not expect, poetry renews with power our weak faith in our destiny. Through the agency of that faith, everything that people do happens.

Poetry releases itself to me in words at the time when something induces in me a state of meditation or song. This something existed before me, is me, and becomes the poem. I follow it blindly.

Now this way, now that, or really, this and that way at one and the same time. As if the heart of speech were to be found somewhere between the mind and the throat, beating to the rhythm of the breath that animates the body, that tense membrane of the senses.

THE GENESIS OF THE POET

I don't remember my first consciously read verse. In our house, Mama was the one who read poetry; sometimes, when something struck her, she would read it aloud. And what struck her was Słowacki, Tetmajer, Leśmian, Gałczyński... baroque metaphors, melodic lines bearing thought soaked with emotions. At the time when I myself began writing (and this was very early on; I was maybe fourteen) it wasn't cool to write so smoothly. What arrived at my ears through the ether was the linguistically knotted voice of Barańczak; on the walls of my imagination hung the shocking images of Wojaczek, and all the girls were interested in Stachura, strumming his guitar... In a word, no sentimentality, and percussive rhythms.

I didn't want to take anybody's side, be in anyone's camp. I wanted to invent poetry from the ground up. And so when I began writing independently, I turned (perhaps in humility) in the direction of the earlier avant-garde: Peiper, Przyboś, Czyżewski, Wat... And here I met up with... form, the hard body of the poem. I poured the female melodiousness, with which my mother had vaccinated me, into manly shapes, which no father gave me (as I didn't know my father), but which I had to create for myself, or inherit from some forebear I'd chosen for myself, or borrow to try out, or steal.

In poetry, form is quite simply words which one uses in such a manner as if one could take them in the palm of one's hand, knead them or break them, and then put them back together in one's own way. It wasn't long before I realised that 'my own way' didn't arise from me at all, but emerged from the words themselves. And so, I was ambushed by form? Yes, but I pounced upon form as well, myself.

As I went on, I felt ever more clearly that writing is not constituted by the lending of one's own voice to foreign, otherwise speechless, words, but, rather, by listening to the words and responding to them. Why write a poem when one knows from the get-go what one wants to say? Then I got my bearings, to a certain degree, in modern poetry, and I could start choosing verses for myself. I was very full of myself, arrogant, aggressive. Yes, I had sparring matches with the shades of poets who approached me at my own invitation. At the time, I wasn't reading like a reader but, rather, like a poet who was scrabbling for his own place in the kingdom of words.

These teenage emotions (which arose from the underbelly rather than the mind) fell away from me only when I was halfway through university. The academy made a cold scoundrel of me, a speculator, a dictator. It was then that I was gripped with the ambition of reading poets from heights above them, and I began to read them coldly, inspecting their technique and evaluating their fitness for my own use. I started to learn on my own — from Herbert, Norwid, Karpowicz... Zbigniew Herbert remained with me for a long time. I was so enamoured of his poetry, that in the end I had to break away from him so as not to be consumed. And yet Herbert taught me a lot — how to think in verse, the use of surreal imagery, the rhythmic precision of words, and above all thinking of 'issues' rather than of oneself. These latter things were transformed within me into a sort of creative technique consisting of the spoiling of one's good humour and a determination not to settle for a given impression.

Then came the time for poetry in foreign tongues — in translation, at the very least. In translation, poetry doesn't reveal itself in the language; it is rather concealed within it and demands the reader to search it out. Some poems can be quite adequately translated, while others can only be explained in translation; still others must be relocated in a different space, or even transplanted like an organic plant to bloom there, to reveal their poetry in a different manner. A poem in translation is like a tempting girl with whom one can fall in love, but never touch.

From foreign-language poets I learned to develop a certain sort of bilingualism in my own writing: speaking in images and sticking out my tongue. I had the sense that through foreign languages I could delve deeper, bidding farewell, of course, to the attractive reflections on the surface of my mother tongue, but for all that, going out to meet some wonderfully alien creatures. To simultaneously satisfy two distinct temptations: that of expected delight and the disturbingly different—is it not this, indeed, which makes us fall in love?

I began to be strongly influenced by Rilke, Eliot, Baudelaire, Mandelstam—in other words, chiefly by the sublime modernists. I was impressed by their philosophical ambitions, for at the time I was also a passionate reader of philosophy. But I didn't write in their style. On the contrary: instead of imitating them in humility, I stole from them barefacedly. I felt justified in doing so, for I believed that a portion of some common treasure belonged to me. There were two anthologies that were great revelations to me: one of French Surrealists and another of the German-language avant-garde. Such poets as Jacob, Apollinaire, Éluard, Trakl, Arp, Goll, Celan... reminded me that, after all, I had always delighted in listening to words, for they set thought in motion, and this enables one to glimpse reality in forms which, without poetry, would be nothing but the chaos of coincidental experiences. I came to realise that what interested me in poetry was inventiveness.

The European avant-garde led me to America next, the poetry of which was fashionable in Poland during my student years. I already knew English verse, but at the time there were quite a few translations of American poetry available as well. I fell into the web of Cummings and Frost, Stevens and Berryman, Bishop and Pound, Auden and Roethke, Ashbery and O'Hara... But Ginsberg, who was so eagerly read by my friends, didn't really speak to me. The Americans taught me that there is no special language to poetry (as there was for the European poet); poetry was, rather, the careful use of the language I heard in my own speech. It was this that provided me with the freedom of speaking in verse. There was no way of tearing oneself away from English-language poetry in those days. The publishing houses were churning out volume after volume of seventeenth-century metaphysicals through twentieth-century American classics and contemporary Irish poets. Thanks to this state of things I came to know Gerard Manley Hopkins and George Herbert, as well as Philip Larkin and Seamus Heaney, none of which, for sure, I'd have been able to read in a profound way with my far from perfect English. From these poets I learned to make use of anecdote and how to compose the process of reading. In other words: the simple narration of refined concepts.

In this way was I conceived. Now the only thing that remained was to be born.

Somewhere at the end of this stream of influences there appeared the Polish poetry of the sixteenth and seventeenth centuries. But by then, I already felt independent, mature enough to consciously commune with the speech of the founding fathers of our common republic. The whole contemporary world mixed in with the old poems of my native language.

Ever since that time I inhabit this vat, inebriated with the beer I brew and screaming at the top of my lungs. Born anew every single day.

ARTUR GRABOWSKI was born in Kraków in 1967. He studied at the Jagiellonian University in that city, where he earned his doctorate, and where he continues to teach at the Faculty of Polish Studies, lecturing on modern literature, poetics, and drama, with an admixture of philosophy, in both Polish and English. He is also director of the Postgraduate Creative Writing Program at that university. He has published nearly twenty volumes of poetry and prose, including dramatic works and literary criticism. In 2018, *Wersje* [Versions], his selected poems, was published by PIW in Warsaw, who also published his latest volume of poetry *Trzy wyspy* [Three Islands, 2024]. World traveller and Fulbright scholar, he has lived in London, Rome, New Delhi, and the United States, teaching at various American universities for three years. He translates poetry from English and Italian, and he has worked as a dramaturge with theatrical companies stretching from Chicago to Tbilisi.

Teresa Tomsia

IF ANYONE'S LISTENING

The verse line opens when I'm rubbing balsam
into my hands, attempting to restrain
the dry skin tissue, which softly—like flakes
of frost—slips out from beneath the fabric
invisible.

I toss about crumbs of my flesh, so they might go
along the well-known road and sink into
the earth—from whence they came, signifying
time passing, time incarnate, time that
times innumerable has sounded in rhythmic breaths,
sometimes in pledges that this greying hair
means little. Petty misunderstandings
hasten no moment on—let this one minute last
which binds us now.

A love poem is an appeal. So let
them blessed be—anyone who shall hear
this particular permission to endure
forever, to crumble inside oneself,
to feel happy—despite the darknesses
and echoes of silence

Poznań 14 February 2024

THE BLACKBIRD WHISTLES

At dawn the blackbird whistled.
Long drawn-out, tenderly, unseen.
As if he were summoning all those
who for life are keen.

Slowly I gather my thoughts—and leaves
wind-tossed last night from the tree
onto the balcony—

impatiently awaiting a sign,
a sunray, the answer of the day
emerging from the dark.

The blackbird's whistle anxiously
echoes, and swells within—Wait, wait,
be watchful, patient—trust.

Soon enough it will grow light
just not right now, not yet.

SOMEONE, SOMEDAY

One of the stories of Angel Rilke
is set in the late autumn, when
the cool of lost moments binds the brow,
the implacable shadow penetrates fragile bone
and letters and e-mails from friends
both close and casual, offer no straight answers.

In any commentary on
what happens near loge and ambo,
it is impossible to find
more sense than that found long ago.

Departing in veils and sorrowing
falling upon knees in the dust
crying out for a lamp with oil.

Erring in the footsteps of the Shadow
on your own path, along which
no one's travelled yet.

A crumbling inside oneself
a falling away from syllables
that someone will arrange
someday.

Teresa Tomsia

BY HIS BREATH

For Artur Majka, author of the painting 'He'.

He set the paint upon the canvas in layers
like soothing balsamed bandages lain
on wounded flesh. Blue. It shimmered
at dawn before in the light it glimmered,
from the labyrinth of lines unspooling the white
smudge of shadow — hardly visible to sight
beyond the curtain — and it grew light.

And then he saw perfectly
that it was finished.

The next day to his studio
he came with a friend.
And the friend was stunned
as it arose — enlivened by His
breath.

2 April 2022

THE WEATHER WILL NEVER BE BETTER

You want to exist?—Poetry has no answer for that.
                    —Maciej Niemiec

The weather will never be any better than it is upon waking.
And suddenly you see—it's worse than it was, and the leaf
that bore the outmoded narrative returns
to chatter on the threshold of the dawn, listening
along with you, ears pricked at questions, echoes, your
        mother's still breathing,
the dog wakes you up at night, e-mails go unanswered.
There have been confessions—mistaken with the hope of
        an enduring
presence, which one so easily takes for a pledge.
In the alley of plane trees, in their ephemeral shade, I breathe
and I am there, where telephones grow silent among them.

There is no better weather or straighter road
and it's well to call to mind once more old matters
stroking what's crouched in the dusty corner
or what's openly passed on to an inner layer.
You exist? Tell me! Tell me in verse,
not in the breath of sleep. The wind tears apart the lungs
with a sudden salty swell—the bitter smell of algae
the sweet aroma of the flesh—united by similarly
unstable matter, formed of clay
truly impermanent.

O poem, tell me, have you preserved
the glance of eyes grown dark, descending
into the depths, suddenly immobilised
like a stone tossed—at the end?

EVOKING ZBIGNIEW BIEŃKOWSKI

I'm sure we'll meet again — in the land of There,
where time is its own master, not us, where Rimbaud
wanders the endless glades.

Participate in everything: beauty and fear.
You must simply go on: there is no farthest feeling.*
Trusting all will be fulfilled again. Spring! Your name
blooms — like May. I'm sure you'd chuckle at the metaphor.
Well, spring sets the head abuzz, and suggests the
    commonest things.

Don't separate yourself from the beginning, which you are,
Don't cover the tracks on the trail you've passed, don't bat
    away the hand
that leads you still. Everything shall be fulfilled once more:
the storks will arrive, the bushes will bud. Words
shall arrive, impossible to express, which must only
be listened to like the wind, then go, not looking back
from the moment that returns us to ourselves — transformed.

I'm sure we'll meet again — in the land of There,
where time wanders the endless glades.

---

* Rainer Maria Rilke, from *Das Buch vom mönchischen Leben.*

A PEBBLE

Today a pebble fell
into my workroom
through the computer window.

I set it on my bench
and inspect it in the light
of Holy Saturday
like good news.

It shines in the sun
flutters its wings
as if it wanted to fly off
to some other home —

but I hold it in my palm
like a gift from Him
who knows what He's doing.

WORDS OF COMFORT

It's good to reflect a bit on one's name-day,
in peace and concentration enjoying my existence
while my patron saint of Lisieux looks on
from above with understanding—
a card with greetings arrives belatedly,
but still and all with the traditional wisdom
that mindfulness is priceless after all.
Should we lose measure between what we know
and what we do not wish to express,
nothing would remain but speechless lips, from which
it's difficult to discern words of comfort.
And still and all, how important is a proper
greeting to each day, especially when
one's conscience is pulsing, wishing to speak out
not only in defence of the oppressed.

Sometimes there are moments like a magnetic
field as when in the foyer of the Dom Literary
I meet Ryszard Krynicki, we greet one another
with a smile saying nothing beyond
what's necessary at such moments Nice to see you ma'am
Nice to see you, sir. We don't draw any closer,
maintaining our positions.
The distance of a few paces is essential,
firmly dividing generations, styles,
editorial boards. It won't be enough:
admiration, sympathy, ideas held in common—
the most important thing is measure.

Warsaw, 10 October 2022.

SKETCH FOR A PORTRAIT

[Teresa, *charcoal, F. Starowieyski, 1991*]

In charcoal sketched, black lines
on grey paper—a sketch for a portrait,
the flesh like porcelain fragile. I might
vanish right now, before I even draw near
the bristol, take it in hand. An hour
therefore, I spend in adoration, as in the world
of vision we found ourselves together
briefly. Soon it too will be
invisible, like the three of us—artist, model,
photographer—and poems.

I contemplate sketches, sculptures
and paintings—to what degree they are able
to transfigure all things, feelings
and the welts I have hidden inside;
deep, permanent. The white poodle inspects
the albums with me, when given a treat
in the corner of the little salon—does he know
that those dark lines mean nothing, that only
this is important—the bright moment
of recollection, a crumb tossed
in the direction of what we call Time?

ON THE RUBBLE PILE

And so my white poodle, off you've gone
into skyscraping spaces, run along then
farther, higher, overleap
the clouds, with an agile jump pass by
the backwoods till in some bright meadow
you find Grampa Bronek—
Legionnaire, Dowborczyk,
tortured to death in the prison camp.

I hadn't the opportunity to get to know him,
my grandfather. They tossed him into a dark pit,
those there, so similar to those who now
stand above a ditch firing at old men,
women and children. I'm constantly searching
for somewhere, and always in vain, to place the oil lamp
on the grave, for someone
to show me the way.

Once more they're stretching barbed wire, knocking
down houses—the bodies dug up, burnt to ash,
nameless, sand mixed
with blood and tears. Abandoned
dogs howl on the rubble pile.

AND SO IT WAS

He used the diminutive form of my name
at farewell—and so it was as if someone
were calling me in from the fields at evening
to supper in the suburbs.

Stay, O moment so suddenly appearing,
let me spread a den for you in memory
where you may hide.

These words—tossed
on slips of paper, written
in green ink, the colour of hope, are
like dried petals today
among leaves crumbled
into shapes illegible.

The only thing they express
is the haste of the hand
that wrote them down, travelling once more
with a portable valise of books
for support.

REMAIN BY THE POEM

Don't scuttle off since you can't
answer, it's enough to approach
closer, lightly touch the smooth
paper skin, follow the trace of the letters
when they pull up at the riddle
of time. That which devours
without responding to any
of your questions.

The poem is like a hand extended;
try to hope that it shall lead
by secret paths, dousing fire-
works, to an open crossing at
unattainable frontiers — you have a friend,
so remain by him, as long as breath lasts
and hearing, as long as you sense the rhythmic pulse
in his arms as you arise
lonely, upwards. Then, unexpectedly,
the curiosity of the ungraspable world
shall come alive.

THE LARCH

For Eugeniusz — along our common path.

With a group of friends, the larch grew wild
at the edge of the park, summer and winter
cheering our eyes, a display of life's vigour when
it greens anew. It's just like how
it is with us sometimes — we support each other
when the big winds blow in,
we keep our promises
we stretch out our arms toward each other
like branches.

Don't say that you won't be any better
after all you know you're becoming
who you wish to be.

A poem is no confessor,
but when you confide in it things
difficult, the worst things, it weeps along with you,
com-passionate, understanding what
you want to change in yourself
and tries to help out —

putting shoulder to stone
along with you and rolling it
uphill.

Poznań, 14 February 2022

Teresa Tomsia   197

WHAT IS BEYOND THE MOMENT

What is beyond the moment of gazing at the sky,
the grey azure sifting mist upon the flat roofs
of the neighbourhood stores, the stumps of skyscrapers
the alleyways with humps to slow down speeders
and the church being built, the lawn beneath the figure
where the dogs leave their piles while
their owners look the other way.

Time gives testimony — once more in parliament
They've held an exercise in diction for our hungering
society, how to out-shout others with the words
'homeland' and 'thief'. The hour shortens: newspaper,
tram-ride to work and back again.

The same hopes as yesterday
that God — since He gave us His all —
ought to be able to weather all this
without having to rely on our grace.

When we are young, we conceive
of happiness as the sum of democracy and skills
acquired in evening school
or on an 'Erasmus' grant — only later
comes the reflection that who we are
in spirit is our greatest measure —
while who it is that's going to measure us
is a whole other thing.

THAT WINTER EVENING

Let us be simple and calm
Like these streams and these trees,
And God will love us and work it
That we shall be ourselves...
                    —Alberto Caeiro da Silva,
                    'The Guardian of the Flock'

If only I knew how to describe it—just that winter
evening, when after supper he drank the bitter red wine
reading aloud the verses of Trakl, wandering the gloomy
paths. Suddenly he stood before me with his shirt
unbuttoned, which seemed unusual, so I went up
closer to see him at least in part the way he had been
created. The hour of farewell had arrived, yet he remained
helpless still, almost defenceless, intent
upon himself, as if he were saying: a man is sometimes lonely
in the face of that which becomes visible.

The light of the streetlamp fell through the window frames
on the sly, screening with shadow our
faces. Lightly I touched arms as downy soft
as rabbit fur and asked in a whisper whether
he'd arrived from some ancient tale? Probably—
he nodded silently, deep in thought, that only
now, when it was time to go and never to return
did I decipher the true name he bears
within himself hiding it beneath his black
sweater, and that even on the beach
he won't get undressed.

If only I could hold onto it, only that one
moment of wonder that—indecipherable in the light
of day—the beauty of existence reveals itself unfailingly
on a December night, and then vanishes, before
I'm able to reach out my hand towards it.

How different with the shepherds in the valleys, as at once
they set out seeing that blazing star on high.

Teresa Tomsia   199

Let us be as simple and calm as trees,
as streams, as those who love without asking,
why them, why we are.

Piątkowo, 24 XII 2023

A POETICAL MORNING

Yesterday I stayed up late to read about 'the match with Real'
in *New Books*, the periodical's still lying
right by the bed; as for the review, although I didn't
make it to the end I grasped that it's not about a game,
but life. I closed my eyes just for a second — and again
it's morning and new games must begin, you can't
succumb to empty lamentations: change mother's
bedclothes, feed the dog, wash the mat by the door
the runner in the room, because Junior the senior leaks
everywhere now, can't make it to the door, and he was such
a good guard dog. Well, no surprise, he's got a tumour in
   his bladder,
survived an operation, had a dozen or so teeth
extracted. The faithful white poodle — now close
to the desk he curls as soon as I start
clacking at the keyboard, as if he knew
I'd be at that business a long while now.

Are words more faithful than animals and people —
uttered, never lost, circling
in citations, thoughts, wandering over paper,
and yet, although repeated — so little
of what is inaccessible do they say.

A DIALOGUE OF DIVERSE DICTIONS

'I was born in a town of displaced persons. / From crumbs of tenderness, from the bright dust of my grandmother's glances / I moulded my childhood on Gomułka Square'. In poetry, the concrete is what is important to me, references to reality, cognitive inquisitiveness, sketches of figures, descriptions of place, sociological and historical contexts. In my poems, I speak of the things I notice in the nearest proximity: people and relations, events difficult to accept but worth describing, that which demands to be noticed. Everything that I see and experience—but also that which I imagine might happen, if not for all the unfavourable existential, social, political, and economic circumstances—these I strive to record in strophes that are at least so transparent as to create something along the lines of an everyday conversation in many voices concerning the significance of the moment, transitoriness and loss, the real history in which our forebears' fates are intertwined: 'Now I know that nothing can be rescued. / There is no more house on the Odra, the Rega, the Warta—/ there is only cunning time; and those more cunning than time / dealers; and the politicians still cleverer than them. And my questions—unanswered'.*

For many years now, I have been led by the envoi of the poet and critic Zbigniew Bieńkowski's 'Introduction to Poetics': 'Lest I should be nothing more than an allusion to myself. / Lest I should be nothing more than a recollection of myself'. I used this phrase in my collection *In the Shadows of Transient Endurance*** as a motto for the poem 'Zbieram chwile na pniu' [Gathering Moments], which opens the volume as an attestation to the fact that the 'community of pilgrimage', the conversation of generations and styles, is essential to me; that I constantly remember Those to whom I owe a debt of gratitude for their inspiration and Whose

---

* From the poem 'Urodziłam się w miasteczku przesiedleńców' [I Was Born in a Town of Displaced Persons].
** Teresa Tomsia, *W cieniu przelotnego trwania* (Poznań: WBPi-CAK, 2021).

mastery I draw upon. For with every phrase I cite, I commence a dialogue of diverse dictions, rousing the strophes to new rhythms.

The first poems that I wrote in my school notebook spoke of the little Pomeranian town full of displaced persons where I grew up in a post-German cellar apartment. A portion of the garden gone to seed was my childhood heaven, savouring of ripe cherries and smelling of lilac. I write of these experiences in the volumes of poetry *Białe tango* [White Tango, 1987], *Skażona biel* [Tainted White, 2004], *Wątpiąc, idę* [Doubting, I Go, 2005], *Gdyby to było proste* [If Only It Were So Easy, 2015] and in my documentary prose: *Dom utracony, dom ocalony* [The Home Lost, the Home Rescued, 2009] and *Świdwin przypomniany* [Świdwin Remembered, 2018]. Firstly, everyday words revealed the things that surrounded us: crates of apples, a doghouse, a bicycle, a kitchen with a wood stove, a tile stove for heat. My sense of existence was based on a loud cry from the hill in a nearby field: 'I am', listening to the echo of the words. Only later, when some real losses began to occur (the passing of young friends, sickness, suffering), and also I began to listen to wartime tales painfully extracted from family memories, did I understand how valuable the spoken word can be, in which what has been lost, what is vanished, what is threatened, can be preserved: the wealth of the culture of my family from the old Eastern Marches, the lost family inheritance of my father with its fragile porcelain and landowners' traditions of hospitality. The poetic phrase soothed the pain of close ones lost and tempered the sadness of separation. The word slowly became a chance to rescue that which otherwise could not be reclaimed in the reality falsified by the censor in the days of the Polish People's Republic; to understand, or to accept. The metaphor turned out to be the one gift of fate that no one could destroy, steal, or forbid: it was a true biography. The word—expressed sometimes only in thought—endured and organised the interior world. The word was my asylum.

My interest in the rhythms of speech began by listening to stories of the prewar past told by my grandmother Waleria, who along with her children had endured six years of exile, having been transported from the town of Słonim near Vilnius to northern Kazakhstan. Her tales, anecdotes, and family legends brightened the harsh existence of families banished in turn from the Tarnopol area (the Iżyckis, Rogalskis, Chałupeks, and Klementowskis) and reignited memories of her heroic husband, the Dowborczyk legionnaire* Bronisław Gołacki, who had been tortured to death in the Soviet gulag camp in Ukhta. He was my mother Zofia's father. Her traumatic fate, in turn, constitutes the theme of many poems and stories, which describe the universal lot of all children wronged by totalitarianism, a question of the virtue of endurance in extreme circumstances, and the value of memory. Twelve-year-old Zosia was transported beyond the Urals and made to work in a kolkhoz. Because she was often ill, she was not fed as she ought to have been and went hungry. Once she bitterly bewept a lost egg that had been given her as a present: 'Today that egg rests upon white paper, / perfect, transparent, a scene of the memory, / which holds the entire cosmos, all of us, / because in it on all sides we are / through and through held captive// We wish to find the lost egg, hold it, caress it, puff upon it, / that it should endure—and take it in hand'. ('Jajko od Kirgizki' [An Egg from a Kirghiz Woman]).

The world revealed, rescued from oblivion, excited me with its mystery, inducing chills of fright, but also inspiring the imagination. I wrote down the family histories I'd heard in a notebook, citing the expressions of guests and relatives, soaked with emotion, which I later set in the framework of rhyme and indispensable repetition so as to preserve the individual inner rhythm of each voice I heard. It so turned out that the notes became something of a satire of those long discussions and the figures of my relatives, so with foresight my father destroyed a few of the first notebooks so that none of our guests should

---

* *Translator's note:* the 'Dowborczycy' were a Polish military formation formed from former Polish soldiers and officers of the Russian army toward the end of Russia's participation in World War One. They derive their name from their leader, General Józef Dowbor-Muśnicki (1867–1937).

be offended if they became known. At the time, I grew interested in short forms—I began to arrange ballads and nursery-type rhymes, which I sang to myself and to our guests during their visits.

A stimulus for the poetic event (the 'lyrical situation' as the literary historian Professor Edward Balcerzan would say, who directed my master's thesis in the Polish Department of the University of Poznań on the 'Discord with the World and Language in the Poetry of Andrzej Bursa') is, for me, usually some moving scene which gives me an impulse to consider the world critically, moving me to delight or protest. It is not written down immediately, but it impels the creative act and the poetic tongue in which I wish to express it. In the poem 'Po raz pierwszy' [For the First Time] this 'concrete', this link with the real world, is a mauled bicycle vanishing beneath the earth. It was buried in a grave along with the boy it belonged to, a grade-schooler, who was riding it when he had a fatal accident on the road. This was an important experience of childhood loss and, only many years later, did I write that the boy 'rode out into eternity / with a youthful passion for the crooked lines / of the first clumsy poem. // My father burnt the notebook in the old post-German stove, / but I believe that the boy's name was rescued from the flames'. The inability to describe loss carries with it a feeling of guilt in the face of the inevitability of transitoriness. For this reason, the metaphor provides us with a wonder-working power of preservation from despair when the person we lament becomes the hero of the poem.

Conversations around the family table taught me that, by listening to stories, we come to know the world and form the style in which we can express the truth we've found, or something beautiful we've thought up, even if we cannot reacquire the lost place of our birth, our home, or our country otherwise than by a domestication of loss. In my poems, I often engage in a lyrical conversation with the poets whose work interests me. It is a conversation about the significance of time and memory, the power of life, and the laws of ephemerality, so as to take up a dialogue and once more decipher what, it would seem, has already been recognised and commented upon. I also return many times in my poetic work and essays to citations from the narrative poems of Maciej Niemiec. He is present in my poetic corpus as a figure — the Parisian Orpheus wandering the alleyways of the city at night — and as the author of splendid poems of struggle against the Void. For this reason, surely, my volume *Liryki przedostatnie* [Penultimate Lyrics, 2022] was described by Professor Magdaleno Rabizo-Birek as a 'dialogue strongly inclined toward others, full of human and artistic empathy'. And that's what I'm most concerned about — a friendly contact with another person and a reciprocal understanding in a language vivified not only linguistically but also in a questioning of the values by which we are animated.

The point of the work is important to me. For example, in the poem 'W każdą godzinę' [At Every Hour], the cry, 'Acquiesce not to silence'. In my poem dedicated to the German translator Renate Schmidgall, I sum up my meditations concerning translation: 'Man is untranslatable / nothing can be done here, except / to constantly set out towards one's own parts, / which seem the most proper / of all, even though the road lead / to the darkest night' ('Przy rzeźbie Rodina' [On a Sculpture by Rodin]).

A personality which allows for a bold contact with the visible world has been of great significance to me along my creative road. I have found a respect for tradition and cultural roots to be very important, along with the code of values passed down to me around the family hearth. The sense of the beauty of the word takes shape from a contact with art, the sacrum of communal prayer at the symbolic grave of our forebears, traces of whom could never be found since the borders of our homeland were changed. The poet Julia Hartwig draws our attention to this marvellously, for example, in the poem 'Portret artysty' [A Portrait of the Artist], in which she underscores the fact that the most important thing is not a question of similarity but a careful consideration and penetration of the wellspring of inspiration: 'whence fell the light'.

In the hands of a poet, words can be a tool for the organisation of the spiritual order, creating harmony and opening out towards other beauties. In a world full of surprises, my poetry tends to be wary, careful of easy phrases and descriptions, and simultaneously interested in the unfamiliar. Every artist moves along his or her own path through the day. Each has his or her own delights in reading, surprises at the twists of destiny, and all of this moulds his or her artistic development and the reflections shared with the reader. The poet has been called a 'bird of paradise'. I would rather compare myself to the magpie who sits on the branch of the fir outside my window—I often see him there—trying to domesticate the surrounding area, preening his white tummy with his black beak, fluttering his wings, shaking the reed of his sharp tail. In a dialogue of diverse dictions, I strive to preserve proportions between what is real and what is imagined, presenting small things, seemingly simple matters, in a world of grand ideas and transformations, which yet return to us a proper measure of endurance ('Okruchy'[Fragments]):

> O, to be such a circus performer!
> To keep one's balance for a quarter hour
> on the tip of a pole—without applause,
> awards, or showing off before the herd—
> on a lonely road following a few fragments
> tossed out upon the path.

Poznań, 3 August, 2024

TERESA TOMSIA was born in 1951 in Wołów. She graduated from the Adam Mickiewicz University in Poznań with a degree in Polish Literature. Besides being a poet, she is an essayist, cultural animator, and the author of documentary prose, scripts, and songs. Her poetry has been anthologised and translated into German and French. She has collaborated with the periodicals *Topos*, *Twórczość*, *ele/Wator*, and others. For several years, she has edited the series 'W pamięci, w odbiciu' [In Memory, in Reflection] for *Fraza*, a quarterly published by the University of Rzeszów. Her most recent publications include a selection of her verse entitled *W cieniu przelotnego trwania* [In the Shadow of Ephemeral Endurance, 2021] and a collection of Parisian lyrics, *W znikającym ogrodzie* [In the Vanishing Garden, 2023], which was nominated for the Orpheus XIII Prize. She comes of a family originally from the old Eastern Marches of Poland, and in her poems, she underscores the importance of dialogue and openness to voices other than one's own. She has been a member of the Association of Polish Writers [SPP] since 1993. She lives in Poznań.

Krzysztof Koehler

FOREIGN BODY

Sight being pure, what was it that I saw?
Girls. Bright faces and the promise of
The evening; all made ready
So festively; groups of young people set
Off into the night, no uprising, no armed
Action, just boys and girls. This night will be
A good night, scent of perfume and promise
Of hugs and rendez-vous; like
The trembling new dawn just before the sun
Comforts the night, like a colt, voraciously
Snuffling the mystery of darkness; or
A sticky bud — a promise of what's to come.
A prologue, anticipating the entrance
Of the actor in the wings, a boxer juking
Before the battle and yet — let it be —
A young man just before he meets his girl,
A groom as the reception's winding down,
A bombardier waiting for furlough gazing
At his wife's photograph, a prisoner
Stretched out upon his cot, a hungry man
Waiting for dinner, a doctor his patient, a nail
A picture.
Sight being pure and wading through
The streets amidst all this I read it all around
Six on a Monday evening. Hypocrite
After all, cramming into my pure sight
A foreign body. I was in no hurry;
Rather, in the Way that falcons have
I searched out just the place
To suddenly reduce the intervening
Space lying between, but from on
High, my sight from far away was
Shifted; I was in no hurry anywhere for sure
The battles had been fought, and long ago
And not at all unemotionally
I gazed at their movements, mimicry, words,
Gestures, which no longer bore me up

Krzysztof Koehler   211

Touching me not. I was like one who looks
In from the other side;
For my dreams had been fulfilled and with them
Life passed on, passed by, and arranged itself
Into something like a long, flat expanse.
Off in the distance a sea of light, but here
A kind of dusk was spread, heavily burdening
The eye. Yes. A heavy sight to bear
And the road home a long one, but
Remembered. For the majority of things
Return to me, like old thumps and
Wounds; like a refrain, like repetitions,
Echoes. I'm the burden, they
Are light. Fulfilment—
Hope. A shape takes
Form in the air
And vanishes at once. I wanted
To tell them something, something from myself,
Sight being pure, which swaddles
Envy and Sadness.
But I said nothing I just
Gaped.

Ash Wednesday 2016–2019

HOUSE ON A HILL

Someone, out of pity maybe, sometime, a dead
Husband maybe (although I don't believe it) or if
frozen in the ditch near the house, and no one knows
what sort of laments the soft snow received;
it wasn't that cold then, the snow was melting, you
couldn't get there. So only later, a neighbour maybe, or
Someone else, how should I know, I'm a
Guest, I'll be gone soon, first time after so many
years of living next door invited past the porch.
I see the masterful workmanship, the felt tiles
(I remember them well from lessons in the old days,
brown, chequered on one side, on the other a smooth
shining surface) nailed tight, so that there shouldn't fall
any dust from above; mud and bran, 'cos they mixed
them here to make the attic ceiling
(I myself once tore them away from the boards
in our loft: a grey shell and dust), when it all dried,
it sifted down upon the kitchen table where
guests were sitting, on bedclothes, paper, people's heads:
Ash Wednesday all year long. There, where tiles were joined
a lath was nailed, flat, rounded, and everything
painted green. 'Your ceiling is green, Ma'am', I said. 'Just
like the whole house'. Bed in the corner, covered with
a blanket, a wobbly table, an electric stove.
A little window above the bed. ''E cum down'
she said, as if explaining for him, ''E cum down
now what yous'r here, but 'e's a good'n, that cat,
'e hadda, 'e's afeared a yous'. Stain on the runner.
A box from the store, flattened, some old throw-rug,
beneath it the tatters of something, a blanket,
a towel? a rag? And then gumoleum.
'It's nice and warm' said my wife, 'An' then 'e got drunk.
I got another room, you wanna see it?
Father was 'ere not long ago. Cris'mas visit
'roun' the parish'. The tiles even lower here.
Wall segments, a little table, doily, candle.
'An' 'e gimme a hwoly pitcher!' A vase

on the table, but no windows, stuffy in here,
mould on the northern wall. 'Do you air the place, Ma'am'?
asks my wife. 'It bein 'so cwold outside?!' She sees
us to the door. Bent double, hobbling on a cane,
her trembling hand on an oaken cane. 'If it wa'n't
f'r 'im comin' roun', it'd be real nice roun' 'ere'.
I don't understand. 'Who'? 'Im!' she says, 'Wot cums 'round
mumblin' anna knockin' onna winder, onna
door, but I ain't after lettin' 'im in 'ere who knows wot 'ed
be up to an...' she's silent. Suddenly. The house
on the hill, the last before the woods, just behind
it, as if somebody lopped them off with an axe,
clearings with the booming river rushing downhill.
As if the visible world ended here.
Right here. As if the openness of fields, balk, paths, deer trails,
as if human roads, as if the sleet constantly
lashed on by the wind, yes, everything that happened
with us, as long ago as you can remember,
as long as streams rush down the mountains, the ice slips
down, as long as anyone's ever thought that he'd
give it another go, although a hard fate jams
him in the earth, in laments and imprecations,
that he'd keep on lifting them legs and despite it
all, take another step, and another, and
the heavens, the stars, the planets and the sun are
constantly accompanying him on
a journey with no end. That's how it seemed to me, that
at this very place we'd hit the shoreline, the edge, the limit
even that slices in half every life, ours as well,
and burns with living fire... A porch, riddled with holes
like a sieve; the snow slips through the cracks, the wind howls.
She stands in the open door, watching us go.
A figure bent double. You can still make out
the face grooved with living. We're on our way, away,
as is only right, every now and then turning
back to cast a glance. The slope leads us downhill.
Behind us just the green of the house. The open door.
And in the door a human figure, bent double. And around her
gloom.

THE ANSWER

Shoes with red laces,
Ragged Adidas from Carrefour,
Step by step, Turkish jeans, under the arm
A blanket roll (because they camped out in the queue
that night) and plastic bags, sweaty bodies,
And a man too with a child in his arms,
On crutches, as he tried to genuflect,
And a grey old man, AK?
Did you see?
Did you see the nation?

I saw them raise flags
Flopping over the Square in Kraków,
How they intoned a song until the windows rattled,
How they searched for a place to crouch before
The Most Holy Sacrament, somewhere
On the far end of the square, inside,
Lifted aloft in the cardinal's hands,
To adore.

I saw, I saw, I saw.

They lit votive lamps and handed round whole
Wreathes of flowers from hand to
Hand, like in a frenzy,
In motion, from place to place,
From the eye of the sky-high camera
Like ants or something with their eyes
Fixed upon the ground.

Don't look at the ground, raise your head to the skies!

Don't look at the ground?
How can I not look at the ground,
Since I am dust of its dust?
Of these sweaty blankets,
Filthy with this standing, smoked
By the slender wick of the candle,
Since I push my way into the crowd,

I see little, for they always cut off the sight,
Come between, I stand on tiptoe,
But still won't even see the jumbotron.
Neither heads, nor shoulders, nor backs,
I breathe, I sing, I weep.

Look up at the skies?
What will I see there?
Of course, a head in the window:
Flashes sparkle in the golden
Frame: commentaries
On group emotion and examination
Of the national conscience: that is
An examination of wounds and wrongs, aesthetic
Chaos and miserable pathos,
A collection of degeneracies.
The demon awoke,
The corpse resurrected,
The demon awoke,
The corpse resurrected
Envenoming, poisoning, Seeping the rot
Of the national slang of the people.
Tfu!

The sky and on it white clouds and an invisible
Paw of dust, which cuddles us, squeezes,
Encloses, leaves us on the square.
Alone.

So it's better to look at the computer screen, a hundred times
The same film and the wailing of sirens
And shots in the misty forest, all the way to
Solutions pinned upon them,
Resolutions, assumptions,
You don't understand, or is it you don't want to,
You're afraid to, understand?

Unruly children are we Lord, to Thee, in the crowd.
Unseeing, seen,
Drawn close,
Lost, recovered,

Befouled, cleansed,
Burnt, crushed,
Toppled, scattered
In powder, dust, and steam.
In splinters.

Firing squads
Honour guards
Artillery salvoes
And a bloodcurdling scream.
And a mumbling through
Tears: O don't forget
Me; don't forget
Me; don't forget
Me; remember me,
Pray for us.

How can I ever forget you,
If I forget you, if I forget,
I won't forget, how can one forget,
I remember I see I hear I am.
I'm in the very heart of it.
I've taken up residence now.
And the grave will not open
Because the grave has not been sealed.

The heaviest gates have been opened.

We're in Poland now.
We're in Poland again.

10–22 April 2010

Krzysztof Koehler

THE TEMPLE

I journeyed 'cross the steppe, that grand ocean (or)
I've even sailed across the steppe, dry ocean (or)
I set out on the steppe, that arid ocean (or)
Surrounded by the steppe, like to an ocean (or . . .)
—Adam Mickiewicz

A fly. The Dawn. The Dusk. A sort
of hill in the background. A poem.
It's possible you never hear
the same sound twice.

That same phrase is embedded there
where circulating blood beats time
imposing sense, although whose sense?
How should I know? And through the door

cracked open grumbles a horse fly,
the hand is waving constantly
as if there was no OTHERWISE
but NO and NOTHING nothing more.

Although 'I sailed out' on those 'depths',
the 'steppe', with birds (cranes?) and Mirza,
the lectern, the hand, and the fly
the forest's edge, my soul and I

all happen once
surely nothing counts
but to lead to a cons-
equence

of simple being and
rhythm: that it has to be
like this, or like it will turn out:
breath: Chatyrdah, burzhan grass, verse.

CHRISTOPHER COLUMBUS NEARS
THE COAST OF AMERICA

Wind. Ever more wind in the hair,
slowly growing stronger you become as dead as
the dawn above the Neckar valley like dusk
in the screeching pines, like—when memory inclines—

the gloomy sun staining the fat-speckled tablecloth
of that summer. The tips of trees, grasses, birds
in flight, smoke—the dreamy signs slip past:
'You'll know yourself in the bitter smoke of fires, secret

escape, the jumbled packing of things'. And so
it happened: if sky, then through the bars
of tree-limbs, and if lovers, then the best option
preserved in clay, sand, mud.

Seen in passing. Touched—already taken away.
Orchards overgrown with mint and herbs. Nothing else;
only the constant transfer to the account in
alchemical gold; limitless contraband—

that this wind, that disturbing movement, is
not to be milled. And that this withering
might yank the horizon into a growing level like that
cry, when the giant flexed: land ho!, land!

Krzysztof Koehler   219

THE PRAYER OF THE LAST COW ON THE PASTURE

Same landscape.
Dogs, echoing bells,
the clatter of a train.
The sun sets and
the crickets fret
the day still,
despite the gloom.

Warmth is friction.
Love is warmth.
Friction steps out upon
the surface of the earth.
Love has twisted this
heaven and hung it
above the fields.
Like a curtain.

Same view.
The return after the great
war to the house
with the wooden porch,
dirty windows
and destruction.

Again in the cage.
The cage imprisons
the voice. Changing
it into grievance.
Grievance is also
song.

Same view.
The last cow
winds slowly about
on its chain. The footsteps
of the farmer growing
distant.

The red and
dirty blue of the sky.
Oh, and the crickets, too.

He'll return. Bounding over
these hills. He'll embrace
the sound. Rub away
crickets, cries,
songs.

Smudging the last
pears and plums
to purple.

The sway of
chains. The prayer of the last
cow on the pasture.
Measured anticipation.
Waiting at the gate.

IN PRAISE OF SCHOLASTICISM

Between the first and the last
Line, on the way of thought from
Grassblade to the King of creation,

Between the bars of the pre-constitutive
Cage to erect fear,
Joy, the might of being.

To elicit the tone. Like a
Flute, God's order
Is dead,
If the player
Stops playing.

KRAKÓW

I raised my eyes as, slowly spilling in
The space of my room so cluttered with things
Softly came purling, like the crystal rush
Of mountain streams, the hejnał from the tower.

Before I'd time to cover my eyes, bells pealing
Accompanied the trumpet, in the dusk
Happily babbling, all the bells there are
In all the steeples of every church there is.

And then — all that remained was an echo,
Like to the distant hum of a far battle
Wafted to soldiers on the wind, tense, waiting
On their fate: joy, fear, anger, and hope...

Krzysztof Koehler

ELEGY FOR THE FALL OF A TYRANT

Once more the crowd wins. The bridgeheads
of tyranny crumble quickly. Past Jasna
Brama, through guards, patrols and
the sublime little turrets of rotary

cannon the mob penetrates
chanting: Rat, rat… The air
continues coughing with shots:
sometimes — dull rumble — a cannonade,

but more often the patter of machine
guns. Heads fall, lightly — like
a beauty drowsing — cables are stretched
before the vigilant eyes of hangmen.

Platoons are marching, rifle to rifle.
Which Spring of the Peoples is this
already? The sun of this age is setting
inexorably, so maybe this is the last

hatred raised a handspan higher,
crime — higher — that head?
Tilted slightly askew now,
swelling lips, peaceful now,

on the tender spool of film, above the entry
gate, shining in the greyish glow
of the windows of our homes.
A triumph, a death mask, a witness or fait

accompli? Interrogation or mere sign,
simply a sign of the times,
a clumsy tribute offered Clio —
the wild epitaph of old Europe.

December 1989

A FAILED, ALAS, PILGRIMAGE TO A CERTAIN PLACE

Through the woods, thick mud
(it had rained earlier),
along the road's edge, and again
along the same road
turning one's back upon
the road-sign with
the name of the town (in which
I was supposed to spend
many days yet)

I ascended the tallest
hill in the area
which doesn't mean — tall:
in proper mountaineering
terms it was a foothill rather,
like — no offence intended — Morskie Oko
compared to Rysy.

I sat down in the arbour.
Archeological remains. Convulsively
pleasant information
on little rectangles:

'magician's den', 'fraudery',
(smoke + fire,
the bloodshot whites
of augurs' eyes), 'temples',

at last: 'Church', 'brothers
minor', for it was they
who received
the legacy of these generations.
The belt of neophytes
bulged here.

I reckoned the hours.
My ear fishing wistfully
for leaves to whisper
catastrophe

Krzysztof Koehler   225

(back then I was
rather skittish, these days
not) or perhaps for
a signal to retreat.

No cannon thundered
nor did any smoke rise.
The defeated slinked
into the woods or across
the sea to other
sands.

Few traces
remain (except
for little signs and shallow
excavations nothing more).
But back then, when the flames
devoured the rest of the church
roof, when the monks

with the Lord in hand
bunged with a cry
the city walls, was
the page of fate
not re-
versed?
And once again nothing reigned but
the sky.

Once more the downpour and
the sodden uniform and
the whole absurdity
of that escape

(just like with those burnt
at the stake
the old faith)
was revealed.

What was I to do,
even with a notebook in hand,
amidst vacationers in the fumes

of boredom,
there up top?
Just one more half-deserter,
half-Levite playing hooky.

MASS AT FOUR O'CLOCK

1.

The bells are still silent. Since
midnight clouds are rolling in and
one hears grumbles. Somewhere
past the mountain the wind's already lurking,
but now the sun is still
holding its glow
and so it remains
as if it were to
last longer than it should —

there's still time, but the old
women are already out on the street
heading to church.
Mass at four o'clock
like the fulfilment
of the second half
of Sunday with the lead
of lonely prayer;
there's still time —
but the old women
are already out
on the street;

the wind's not yet blowing
and the sun is scraping the
asphalt desperately as if for the last time,
and yet there's still time,
because Mass is at four
and nothing extraordinary
has to happen, old women
filling the afternoon full
with their shuffle to Mass —
that Sunday soap opera
they've been airing for two thousand
years now and will continue to air
as many (how many?)
years
as it takes, so many one

can hobble along calmly hobbling
to the door before the wind, before
the rain, before the thunder; make it
before,
get there,
hobble in.

2.

Peeling wallpaper, rickety doors,
a stove, family photos, laces, curtains,
Krakowiaks
on the windowsills and overtightened locks
tsyktsyryktsyk
as if they'd slipped out from under avalanche,
skirted cataclysm, escaped flood
setting out on wobbly boats
onto the broad river from narrow feeder streams;
ah, how that burly river overflows its banks,
flooding the street, knee-high, belt-high, an element, and
whole trees sliding by in the current, rubbish,
woodshed drawers rinsed clean by the cataclysm
colourful magazines
quite a few naked ladies, tattered, what
is hidden is revealed, what's revealed is
lost: earthquake, flood,
pestilent air.

3.

And spare us: spare us, spare us,
from,
rescue us,
slip us in your breast-pocket, up
your sleeves, mufflers, hide us
deep, let our eyes, terrified
not sweep the cracks in the hospital
wall, let no rattle of pails awaken us
at mealtime, let us not be covered
by the fear of what might happen, let
nothing happen at all, which should
wring the neck of our life, let
nothing happen if possible, nothing at all,
nothing, nothing; so that we should no longer fear,
so that we should not be consumed with fear.

Krzysztof Koehler

And then he asked me if I
saw how the earth just slipped
away!
So I told him yes,
that yes, I saw it, cracked
foundations and nothing to do about it,
women running around with cries and
that first it was the earth that slipped away, then
the roof collapsed and that which had been hidden
(ah, those water stains above the stove and traces
of the capers I shared with my wife,
her footprint on the ceiling, this sort of
sign of ours), was revealed. And
you saw us there, as if naked,
uncovered, handed over now, but the rain
wrapped its eiderdown round us; and we were
inside, forever again already.
And I told him, but not everything,
because I heard a crash, then a bang, as if
the earth were slipping away, I thought
it's over now, there you have it, and I saw that roof,
crash, an ordinary crash.
It was sort of set aside.
And it was already readied
as if in destiny's hand,
you saw us, yours,
handed over, stripped,
suddenly subject.

5

Even when no storm is on the way,
expect the thunderbolt, the thunderbolt!
'I tried to get back in time,
my daughter came in from the city,
and her train drowned out the hammering
of the thunder, and her hammering at the door
the first drops;
we plucked a few flowers, gillyflowers,
cornflowers, and those that grow near the well,
red hollyhocks and with them

we went, Ave Maria,
to church, bearing flowers
Stella Maris, and later to the grave.
'O bright Star of the Sea!
O haven of the shipwrecked,
the waves now wash over
our prow'.

6.

And if now nothing, at least
the crickets and the flies
because something's about to happen
anyway not much will remain
from speech, tatters, phrases
torn, not at all those
composed according to rule,
but coincidental, blurted,
ah, rescued, not at all like that, not
those, which were supposed to be rescued,
those remained like stones
poking above the current so
don't be waiting on something here
to come to fruition chance
or destiny, or fate,
nothing will happen,
everything will happen,
whatever will happen
will be as given
not what you wanted,
not nicely arranged,
tumbled about
or lost:

but you've still got
a lot
of
time
till four

July–August 2006

THE METAPHOR WILL TAKE YOU IN HAND

Illusive comfort! That it'll return
To the root, nourishment for
The titmouse, defence of nests!

These histories are to
Create the end! Stories,
Assumptions, legends,
Epics.

The metaphor will take
You in hand. Now
It shall rock you
The inevitable and
Hyperbolic
Will nestle you to the void.

A lonely stump that
Once was a tree.
A stick stabbing
the sky sucked clean.

Blackened. Barked,
Habitation of bugs,
Woodpeckers' pantry.

It was to be like a challenge
Packed in symbol.
Lulled in
Humming;
Corseted
With comprehension.

A corset.
Like
A corset.

PROFESSOR TOMASZ W. ASKS TO BE
REMEMBERED IN YOUR PRAYERS

Those skinny ankles poking from his shoes and
I had a question on the tip of my tongue about common
Ancestry. Stanisławów, the turn of the century,
and that there mixing up of peoples and nations.

Socks pulled up, hidden the skinny ankles
poking from the shoes, as if they were to reveal
Some not at all vanished aristocratic spirit.

Articles moused through and poems collected
For a new anthology, up to his neck in a life
Of labour; and maybe even a trip to Bulgaria
After the season, when the fruit is ripe and the water warmer.

And banal associations. Attempts at describing life
     burning down.
Plotting to outwit the triumphant progress of cancer or
     coronal
Disease.

He remains in his books the naive ones coo,
But the methodologies have changed, today one doesn't
     write like that
any more, so he's gone.
Modish discourse won't shield him.

He's gone off to the shades, and with him that which had
     followed him,
Wife, children, something that certainly soured
The length of days beyond worries of the next paydates.

They were never here, how can one decipher them from
     skinny
Aristocratic ankles, and going further, can one
Describe those ankles poking from beneath the eiderdown
As he embraces his wife

No, I won't go there. The only thing is I can't
Forget Professor W., with whose family perhaps
The Koehlers had something to do in Stanisławów at the
     turn of the century.

Krzysztof Koehler   233

But that's not it either, it's not about an intersection of lines
But the question that grows with age:
And becomes like the despairing shriek of a lost child;
Giving birth to fear when it appears, throttling the throat
With its frigid hand on sleepless nights.

That I don't know why he lived and that I'm following in
   his traces
so closely.

Oh well, skinny-ankled Professor W. is dead.
His body's probably rotted away in the grave long ago.
   He's gone,
As if he never had been, and perhaps after his fourth book
   published
He grasped what I only grasp today, perhaps after twenty
   some years.

But that knowledge just makes one's calves tremble.

But why does it bother me, since so many other nearer
Dearer ones have bit the dust?

I don't know. Close the book already.

WHAT IS A POEM?

1. WHAT IS A POEM?

An ordering of words arranged in a certain pattern (determined by the will of its creator), which fulfils the basic function of language.

For ages now attempts have been made to determine the certain characteristics that distinguish the language of poetry from the language of, for example, prose. What is more, for ages now (in these latter ages rather than formerly) creators have been to a certain degree successful in blurring said distinguishing characteristics on behalf of the demands of liberty and unfettered creative expression, through normative recommendations in which they resemble simultaneously the famous protagonist of Cervantes and Baron Munchausen: for poetry is conventionalised artificiality after all, and to contradict this is like setting off to battle with windmills, pulling oneself out of a pit by one's own hair. For ages again (these latter, not those former), literati have suffered from this affliction. Of their own free will.

2. WHAT CAUSES POETRY TO ARISE?

As I see it, poetry is set in motion by an interior need, a sort of pressure, which demands ex-pression. For if one writes poems only 'rarely and unwillingly' (the first statement is objectively true, the second is certainly due to some temporary distraction of the author of these words), that only means that said pressure is not of permanent duration.

3. WHENCE COMES SAID PRESSURE?

God only knows.

But so much can be said, that inspiration (and there are as many inspirations as there are inspired) must be distinguished from the 'need', 'will', 'desire', 'necessity' of writing a poem.

For, as I see it, all people experience a certain inspiration to thought arising from reality (whether interior reality or the exterior reality that faces them), but not all people (or rather, only a negligible percent of people) experience the need of setting down said inspiration in written record ordered in a certain pattern (vide §1 supra).

4. WHO THEN IS THE POET (THE POETESS, THE 'PER-
SON CREATING POETRY', ETC., AND SO FORTH)?

Well, of course it is that person (etc.) who, having expe-
rienced inspiration (to think about something), brings his/
her hands down upon the keyboard or grabs the felt-tip pen
and begins blackening a sheet of paper. A rag by nature and
custom as white as snow enslaved. A white flag of resignation
from future struggle.

5. STRUGGLE? RESIGNATION?

Well, certain things aren't comprehensible by one train
of thought. Certain things—the colours and sounds of a
spring morning, the aroma of fields warmed by the sun, or,
for example, that 'swaying into openness' of Martin Heideg-
ger's, let's say—initiate a process: they speak something to
us, very strongly, but... unclearly. As if they were mumbling,
and we couldn't suss out to the end what it's all about or
why it sparks such emotions in us. Both poets and poet-
esses (persons etc.) are those who don't just shrug at such
moments (as do the majority of us; that is, the majority of
us remain at that stage of first impressions, intuitions, but
we do not follow these any further in order to extract or to
understand, to grasp or comprehend in images what it was
that 'struck' us). And they, the poets, poetesses, etc., don't
shrug, they follow.

6. SO IN WHAT WAY ARE THEY DIFFERENT FROM
THINKERS? PHILOSOPHERS?

First, because they do what they do in a different sort of
speech (vide §1 supra), and secondly, because basically they
don't clarify what was going on during the stage of said
inspiration, rather, they enliven that inspiration, endowing
it with long endurance, which in the case of great poets,
poetesses, etc., is even eternal. Capisci?

7. NO, NON CAPISCO. TRY HARDER.

All right. So there's this poet R. M. Rilke. And he's sitting
or standing in some museum gaping at an 'ancient torso
of Apollo'.

8. OK, AND SO?

And so he's looking at that monument, that sculpture, and something starts churning inside him. He doesn't know what. Some sort of dark, fundamental experience. But what? He doesn't know. Something strong, something primordial, which goes beyond aesthetic contemplation. He feels, perhaps, that what he's looking at will change his life, or shape it, or—the absolute beauty of this sculpture somehow annihilates him, smashes him to smithereens, pulverises him. He's trembling all over. But he doesn't know. Because he's not a philosopher, just a poet (and if it matters, Rilke was a male person, historically speaking). And he writes a poem about this. About this moment. He records his sensation...and provides us with the opportunity of participating in this sensation of his. In other words, in allowing himself to be inspired, he draws along our consideration, but what it is that remains in this poem is that moment at which he realised what was going on, and when he finally begins writing (this is how it sounds in the Polish translation by Jastrun), 'every inch of this stone sees you / you must change your life', and in this way he creates his poem. Because, in the end, he switches directions: it's not me looking at the marble, it's the marble that's looking at me. And it's 'his' gaze, not mine, which is transformative of me. Despite the fact that the statue in question has no head. Or eyes for that matter. But that which was capable of expression in that moment, when the poet felt something of that sort, at this moment now takes hold of us, touches its readers, allows us a shared experience.

9. WELL, ALL RIGHT, BUT WHAT IS IT THAT THE POEM GIVES?
?

10. WHAT DOES THE POEM BRING?

Can you speak more clearly? What's it supposed to bring? And to whom?

11. TO HIM FOR EXAMPLE, WHO'S READING IT.

Nothing measurable. Maybe an admiration for the poet's skill. A wonder at his ability, at the proper choice of words, the intriguing metaphors, or the surprising fact that something as banal as a boiling kettle can be considered in the manner that Marcin Świetlicki describes it in his famous phrase 'Fuckin'-a boil a'ready!' He's speaking here to the water, the lyrical subject, that is, because he wants the water to boil already so that he can make the tea, so that She could drink it and go off already 'into the gloom', in short, be off already. It's a very surprising perspective, that. And I could probably give a thousand examples of what sort of power there is in poetry! The power of eliciting a cognitive dissonance. The portrayal of an unusual perspective or the casting of a surprising light upon people, things, or situations. That's poetry.

12. AND THE POET? WHAT ELSE DOES THE POEM BRING THE POET?

a. Nothing more than that, for sure. He comes to learn more than he knew before he sat down to write the poem. Those poems are the best. Successful ones. Poetry, please believe me, often surprises its own maker: the end creation brings a surprise to its creator.

b. And in the same way poetry (the successful poem) brings its creator great joy. The poet derives a great satisfaction from the successful poem. In other words, the fulfilment spoken of in §12.a. The poet who is fundamentally satisfied, who derives satisfaction from the poem begins to yearn when he finds himself in a situation when he is not writing poems (and such times are much more frequent than when he is writing 'rarely and unwillingly', vide §2). The writing of verse is an addiction to such moments when the poem succeeds. One would like to repeat such moments. Because poetry differs from prose in this: in bringing my statements to an end, I return to §1: the writing of verse is not a desk job. The immediacy of reception is equal to the brief time of its creation. We now have the poem and we experience joy or satisfaction at the fact that we were capable of writing a good poem, but then the time arrives when we are not writing a poem (because this is no desk job), and we begin to yearn for a repetition of that state of satisfaction or joy... and we give it another go. And we keep trying like this until we die, because the writing of poems is necessary to one's life.

KRZYSZTOF KOEHLER is a poet, essayist, historian of literature, and a renowned expert of early Polish culture. He was coeditor of the periodical *brulion* and has authored nine books of poetry, including *Obce ciało* [Foreign Body], his collected poems from 1989–2019, published in 2019. Besides this, he has written a critical study of Stanisław Orzechowski, a biography of Piotr Skarga and an essay on Renaissance-Baroque culture in Poland (*Palus sarmatica*, 2016). He is a professor at the University of Stefan Cardinal Wyszyński and has also taught at Jagiellonian University, the Ignatianum Academy in Kraków, and various universities in the United States. For several years, he played a major role in the propagation of Polish literature abroad, serving as the director of the Polish Book Institute.

Wojciech Kass

A LITTLE METAPHYSICS

Riding into town from the forester's lodge I succumb to
    the illusion
that the road I'm travelling runs downward
and when I'm returning, that it rises up.
Actually, I'm travelling neither downwards nor upwards.
These are lowlands after all, and, as they say, meandering ones.
Even so, this undermines in no way my little, local
    metaphysics.

I WAKE UP FROM THIS DREAM RUNNING

A room bathed in rays of sunlight
as if angelic linens were hung out there to dry—
linens of transparent gold.
I hear their voices in the kitchen:
mother, father, a neighbour woman
bringing in gossip from the street
like spring vegetables, cheese and fresh rolls.
They don't wear glasses yet, no asthma nor cough torments
    them.
Full of laughter and smiles
they like their cigarettes, strong coffee, and scrape together
    pennies
for the weekly hand of cards.
I throw off the covers and run towards them
in my sleeveless shirt, with the little bells of my genitals
like a lamb rushing to the flock
above which the warm steam rises
from islands soaked with monsoon rains.
Mama, Papa, Mrs Renia!
I want to leap onto their laps
but instead of my father's strong neck in my arms
on my cheek instead of my mother's ear with its cold spark
    of earring
there's nothing.
I fall into an abyss
and I wake from this dream running, but not weeping with
    a boy's tears.
The tear, which doesn't fall just now, will be discovered later.

CRABS

The dream that returns like the tide,
in which there's always the same port,
captaincy, docks, scaffoldings
and boats with furled sails rocking.
They lack only shipwrights, helmsmen, oarsmen.
They are somewhere else, as can be seen from this dream,
sprawled in linen shorts
drunk on wine and tanned by the untimely sun
like crabs tossed on shore by the sea.

THE SONG OF MY WIFE'S BREATHING

Waking at 3:55 I swallow words
like a bird swallows blackthorn sloe:

Angel of God my guardian dear
to whom God's love entrusts me here,
ever this day be at my side
—that's all I can remember.

I hear her soft breathing.
Her breath that I would take into my beak like water
and carry away without letting a drop fall,

which I'd cradle in my beak
like olive oil in a lamp and carry so
that the rain should not douse the flame,

that I'd carry like a dried
apple, pumpkin seed, barley grain.

And when do I hear her breathe? At night.
And when do I see her breathe? When it's cold.

Don't flutter off, little prayer.
Your tiny, ancient words are like chicks

I'd gather with my own beak like blackthorn
and carry off into the pergelisol
beyond the glacier.

Angel of God keep under your care
my night, our, night. My cool and hers.

Be vigilant to help people
tonight, in this cold.

THE CENTRE OF THE BED

I think of the view past the window
into which I fall directly upon waking;
of the yard: hawthorns, jasmine, oak
and why do I see ever less?

Because I open my eyes at a distance,
closer to the edge of the bed.
When I embraced my beloved
I saw more, sunrises as well.

SONG OF THE HOUSE ENLARGED

In the bathroom, in the bed
In the kitchen with its view
On the feeders for tit, jay
In this big house
Where we meet up night and day

In the cellar, in the larder
At the door with its view
On the lake of herons, garganeys
In this big house
Where we meet up night and day

On the stairs, in the attic
In the arbour with its view
On the woods of deer, badger
In this big house
Where we meet up day and night

Past the windows, past the doors
Where we mill the quotidian mist
Cloudlets engraved of light
In this big house
Where we meet up day and night

In the chimney, in the hearth
Where we light a stump of fire
Like a beech-log breviary
In this big house
Where we bear our sooty love

In the curtains, paravents
Where we rake our daily filth
Drafts from frost, puffs of rime
In this big house
Where one day we'll greet our death

Day and night unfathomable
of lime, shroud, and kisses

SONG FROM THE WINDOW

Trees of the wilds, why such strange trees? The trunk grows
upward, branches stretching upward and to the sides, here
     bare there
in needles, and over there in buds and leaves.

Cats, why such strange cats with tails stiffly
upward, and on four paws?

Man, who needs such a strange man kicking about with
     a spade
around the circuit and pushing a wheelbarrow of sawdust?

Smoke from the campfire, whence such strange smoke
     from the campfire censing
spruce and pine?

The shadow of chimney smoke, what's up with the shadow
     of smoke and the chimney?
A moment ago it was smoking on the driveway from which
     snow was cleared
onto the lawn, and now it's shifted right and is smoking on
     the lawn,
from which no snow's been cleared onto the driveway.

Garage wall, who needs such a strange garage wall which
punches holes in the sun, while shining whiter than snow
     making the
onlooker squint?

Why the strange chap who squints his eyes in the window
upstairs and says:—Nothing is strange?

Strange?

KINGLETS

Oak tree rooted in my poem, or maybe not you
but your neighbour oak, and maybe not a poem
but a dream in which you were like eternity
constantly growing, unfathomable to the pilgrim.

Shelling the acorns in your crown I saw no
beginning or end, top or bottom, nothing
that swayed or flickered, sprayed or hid away,
while amidst the thickets of light I erred like a child:

from what twig swells the bud, the twig
from what branchlet, the branchlet from what branch
the branch from what limb, the limb grows from what
trunk, the trunk from what underground root,

and the root from what rootlet's mouth sucked the first
sip of juice, and the rootlet from what seed sprouted,
the seed in what clod burst discarding its shell?
In what part of the dream are You found, in what part I?

And falling, do you know how our falling takes place:
in the crown or crownless? In the crown or beyond, where
nothing sways or flickers any more, nothing sprays or hides
away.

SPARE NOT TO STROKE THE DYING

For Weronika L.

Stroke the dying
Head and arms
As you stroke a cat
Asleep, not to death.

To sleep and not to die
To wake like a child
Stroke me Mama, O, here
So I should dream, not die.

Stroke the departing
Views for eyes that no longer see
Sounds for ears that no longer hear
They shall be warm as they die down.

They shall be warm as they die down
Like the fur of beast, the grass
O yes, stroke me like that
So I should wake and rise.

That I should rise and wake
Stroke my face and arms
So you should rise from bed with me
Having died but perished not.

Wojciech Kass   251

AT DEPARTURE

My mother puts things away:
forks and knives, dishcloths, napkins, pendants
from table to drawer, from shelf to stool
from sill to chest, and later
can't find: spoons, combs, tubes of stuff.
My mother's brain squirms, absorbs, breaks down,
turns away from all without.
You're naughty, you Devilish Without — she says
for stealing things: forks, cotton, pins.
And despite it all my mother leaps up:
she wants to go outside, to the park, to the store
(in her hand she's gripping hanky, pendant, keys),
she wants to go out to the German-speaking tourists,
she wants to go see her sister in Oliwa, her cousin
on Chopin St, she wants to go visit
the demolished house of her neighbour lady
remembered from childhood, razed in the seventies,
that wanders through her dreams like a tatter of shiny fabric.
She wants to go see her brother Gerard's grave on
    Malczewski St
and move towards those things, those what-you-call-its:
spoons, forks, combs, pins,
bags, parasols, and keys.
Where is it I want to go, son? — she asks.

PEACHES

At summer-zenith, when the light begins to overripen
(can light overripen?) when the peach
is a condensed drop of sun, a sweet
solar tear, we bade farewell to the cremated dust.
Our silhouettes were thrown against the marble
plates of the columbarium—as if on a mirror
black and polished.

What was that funeral for, what, that summer-zenith, the
    orchard
of sweet sun-tears, if not that I might pose
for the first time a question to the ash
—a fundamental one,
as it invokes edible light—
Ah, my cremated one, my
departed, did you like
peaches?

GREY HAIR

Don't say
you don't have them

from your stray grey
hairs

you might
wind a nest

for a linnet

DOORS

For Wiesław Uchański

Nothing's ever opened
by heart-choking fear
so who are you hoping
to see as you stare
at those closed doors?

Great winds bang and stream
through mysterious dreams.
Who are you waiting for
eyes locked on those blocked
doors?

A hundredfold abyss
attacks you; again
the lock rattles, you hiss
with pain, but don't press
the key so tightly in your hand.

This life is much more
than mere breathing. Remember:
the knock came at the door
but you trembled
and turned away once more.

One tomb overcome
in that Tomb bursts the dawn.
And yet how many scores
of us died, the far side
of closed doors?

Wojciech Kass

SILENCE

From the columns
of gazettes chased off
the verse.

Under homey
thatch kicked
the verse.

In Warsaw salons
ridiculed
the verse.

A dunce's cap
jammed on
the verse.

Before parliament
impailed
the verse.

By pigeons
in Lwów beshat
the bard.

The clochard
for a dram declaims
the verse.

A bomb
in the heart of the loony
the verse.

To the clinic
to be euthanised
the verse.

At you, worm,
is pointing
the verse.

MEDITATION 30.

i nestled close
to the bruised

bespattered Body
of Jesus Christ

tenderly pressing up
against the sacred Flesh

covered in wounds
scabs and blotches

battered and swollen
befouled to the bone

just after having
cleverly slipped into

the grave before
Joseph of Arimathea

rolled up the boulder
that sealed off the exit

and while I was stroking
the foul-smelling hair

of the helpless god
stiff with blood and sweat

like currycomb bristles
came the third day

and we rose again
from the straits of death

and for that reason healthy
in body and mind I can

offer you these apocrypha
of the most beautiful

sleep
i ever had

Wojciech Kass

THAT FROM THE DEAD

She dreamt she went downstairs, opened the door
and entered the morning, the peace of the garden,
that on the table near the porch a bee-eater sat,
a parrot on the arm of the wicker chair,
a blue roller on the branch of the mulberry, and
the oriole dead for ages fluttered close, a finch
was preening its feathers on the old root
and that other birdlife — colourful and exotic —
stood round the garden singing one by one
except the finch, who kept tousling his wing,
they sang what they had to, needful, needful
and immediately, needful in a perfect way
that from the dead, that the living arise,
that the flashing silverware, the pulsing curtain,
the shiny satin, the splash of miracle
the drizzle of things massed together, that nothing was missing
Nothing.

WITH A VOICE THAT KNOWS NO BOUNDS

There was a fish a loach in the lake and a girl
sewing chasubles with gold and ruby thread
there was a lifeguard who said: ice, and below the ice
water, there was a grande dame—asleep on the sofa
who said 'yes' to someone who stopped by in her head;
there was this bell in Sandomierz and a tree, a boulder,
and none of these abandoned one another, there were
    chestnuts
on a certain street and a certain mother, aged
and streetless, there was a red eye and a mewling cry
neither evil nor petitionary of a grey gull on a step;
there was a raw cliff in February light
on which a noble sketch of naked birches;
there was a warehouse built on a dune, a little wall
with a view to rail sidings and a wall made firmer
by boyish hands with a mortar of mud; there was a little
    donkey
who heeded one person only, my great-aunt;
there was a flickering light in the gardens, there was glass
in the ground and beneath it silver candy-wrappers, there
    was a peartree
as slender as a mast, and beneath it a dog's grave; there
    was a stair-
-well inhabited by the aroma of apples wintering
in the cellar; there was a bald parrot in a cage, a jackdaw
clutching a walnut; there was a little flock of serins
on the sandy firebreak, there was a little fisherman's boat
in front of the preschool with yellow, blue, and black
stripes, with a number on its stern that no one,
literally no one, remembers, there was a hill like a nón lá
Asiatic hat—thus I saw it walking along the spine
of a range—with a blond braid of paths at the summit;
there was evening on the verandah, evening self-absorbed,
and a poplar spreading stillness from within, and from within
a radiant sadness; there was Dora adored
by a basketball player known as Cod for he had eyes like
    a cod;

there was Żulek, Lola Colt, Berka, Lun, Edy Polo
and one, one and only volume of verse borrowed
from the library, there was milk fragrant of sunwarmed fields
now walloped below the tomb of the housing estate; there
    were poets,
the first entered into a relationship with the Visible,
the second gave his heart to Abstraction, the third married
    Big
Bertha Irony, who used to tell one and all how to weave
stories of the world, and the fourth lacked talent enough
to satisfy his ever-randy wife Deconstruction,
there was a fifth called the Idiot, for he only chased
after the tail of his own poem, constantly, there was a dream
in which he dreamed his wife another woman like another
marigold; there was the hand of the stonemason set on
    the gate post
of rough granite; there was a walk along a beechwood path
    with an old
writer; there was a belt-loop of calf-leather, a hoopoe
dipped in paint as red as blood; there was a rope
dangling from a wagon-shaft; there was an elk all in a cloud
    of gnats;
there was such a moment and a disinheritance therefrom;
there was a golden bumblebee mislocated in the middle
    of August
in a bouquet of tansy and spindletree. There was me;
and I didn't even notice when I died, and you,
ring, little bell, the hips of the night have just shimmied;
there was a light flickering in the gardens and an innumerable
amount of information needed by no one
not even worth sneezing at not
worth a pin.

SPECTACULA

the darkness of neons
the darkness of adverts
the darkness of screens, monitors, and cameras
the fluorescent darkness of laboratories, offices, headquarters,
the darklybright eyesoaping of intellectuals
the politically dark cul-de-sacs, the dark trees of tomorrow
moth-ashy dark of dilettantes who
know everything, everybody
that is to say nothing, no one, light-haired
dimness of celebrities, modistes
the resplendent darkness of achievements recorded in
Guinness, the obfuscation of milling tongues
the gloom of brutal facts
the celebratory pushiness of the LED-
flickering glittering shit
above the poles of night
the tomb of the moon.

FROM PSALM 59 (58). FODDER

The artificial light of illuminations, lanterns, neons,
     windows, fizzles
And they are constantly growling in the night in search of
     entertainment.
They are like a tribe of jackals.

And should they not tear apart some being, or tear apart
     some thing,
Then out of boredom they shall howl at the drum of the
     moon (O how sweet at times her figure)
And then run breathless into the desert (ah, mean and
     cursed the bitch).

AND THOU SHALT DWELL IN DESERT PLACES

For Wiesław U.

If you want to know what your poems are worth,
go into the desert and pitch your tent in the place
where her heart is fixed, dry and pumping sand.
Get up each morning and stand ramrod straight
at attention and read. A month later
you'll throw the book away,
for you will know your poems by heart.
You will still not know the desert
but she will remember you. Be prepared for the worst.
If no miracle happens your recitative will be
like the spilling of sand from your mouth
into the mouth of the desert.
In this way you'll arrive at the desert.
But if your feet sense the earth trembling
which may herald the approach of caravan
or three-humped camel,
if a lizard should scramble up to and under your tent
and at least one blade of grass should sprout
an herb as pale as the hair of your head
you will have proven your words.
But what if none of this should happen?
Then the entire desert will pass through you
transforming your existence into its own song.
A song of sand.

A LULLABY OF RUSTLES

you hear falling
a sliver
of sharpened pencil
a fingernail clipping
the head of a match

or Icarus.

ATTENDANCE

I dreamt that the class roster was being called:
Iwona Bobrowicz, Janek Bober, Zdzisław Dyszkant,
Grywacz, Kass, all the way to the end of the list
all the way to the back benches
and all of us answered: present.
And who is absent?
—Everyone—I heard
a voice say, a voice that belonged to none of us.

WHICH IS WORSE

Once more the earth needs pure water, air,
her innards filled with oil, noble ore,
healthy elements; trees must be planted
many oaks, lindens and spruce, pasque-flowers
lilies of the valley, and then leave the woods alone
so that they might return to their
mother, for what is architecture anyway, asks the poet,
if not the monkey's yearning for the wilds? Our earth
needs its lost butterflies, birds, and beetles returned
to it; catfish and rudd to its lakes, to its seas
the lamenting dolphin — they were deities once,
the dolphin and the roaring tiger — tear not away
from our sister bees their pastures, nor fields rich in nectar.
Are we no worse than our forefathers? You think?
We are so much less innocent, we are refined
in our crimes, we are elegant in inventing
instruments with which to commit them, and aims
for the havoc we execute, which is worse.

THE BUOY

The day drowses. With half-closed lids the dusk remains
    vigilant
And the campfire, in which I burn remnants of
    dissatisfaction, adding them like lumber.
In the reeds there are boats like dogs in doghouses. The
    screech of the tawny-owl,
On the horizon which is no final station voiceless stands
    the caisson of the night.
And you, bathing, swim towards the shore, your head like
    a buoy. Black.
I stir the last flames with a stick. Believe me, tomorrow a
    new world shall arise from this,
If not a better or worse one, then the the same sort of
    one. Without us. With us.

Wojciech Kass   267

TO A POET UNKNOWN, ON PLANET WORD

Thousands of pages have been written about the relation of the poet to the word. Still, gentle Sir, you will do me a great honour if you allow me to take advantage of our correspondence and toss my own three proverbial cents into this so essential matter, offering my own particular recipe. As I have already mentioned, no such thing as a recipe for the writing of poetry exists, and still and all, countless numbers of the same are bruited about. Who would dare count them up? If ever, dear Sir, you should come across someone who stubbornly insists upon his or her possession of the key to poetry, dighted in some article or another, it would be best to send that worthy gent or dame packing off to hell, yea, to Beelzebub himself, with a dunce cap firmly jammed over the ears. Józef Julian Sękowski, a controversial Romantic who came into the world in 1800 in Antagołany (near Wilno), described a 'diabolical breakfast' consisting of classical literature and philosophical works, in his novel *An Interrogation at Lucifer's*.

As for my three cents, here they are. Words are much, much older than we. And the representatives of the elements, flint for example, are older than words. Flint in hand (and thought, thought too: What on earth am I supposed to do with this?), man began his journey to civilisation, arriving at last at that stage of technology based on flint flakes. This stone, dear Sir, is a deposit of matter and energy together — ergo, a thing both material and immaterial. Enchanted in its flinty bowels lies the elusive element of intelligence (this was communicated to me not long ago by the artist Rafał Strumiłło). Besides flint, there are other bodies, organic and aetherial, and precious metals that are important, even timber (with one condition: that saws must never bite into it: we must allow it to root in the soil and tangle its branches in the sunlight).

Words are older and greater than us today, as they contain meanings bestowed upon them by our forefathers, meanings which evaporated from them over the course of the ages, for the life of the spirit and all spiritual ceremonies adjacent thereto, now more quickly, now more slowly, are set aside by so-called progress, classified under the heading *inutilia*, in which neglected drawer they waste away, assuming the form of mere shells without content. Just imagine, my dear Sir, how many human beings spoke before you began prattling as a babe, making use of words we still utilise, acting thanks to them, and with them constructing identity! The word links us with our ancestors, leading us into conversation with them. The word remains an instrument of cognition and the description of the times in which lived those who have now passed away. In the word, we find the thought and symbols of those times, the ideas and programmes, yearnings and dreams, prophecies and phantasies, more or less clearly stamped. Man scars over with the word, and in the word there remains the impression of this scarring: of the individual and the community, of the tribe and the nation, of societies and peoples, of city-states and global powers, of islands and continents. Let us remember: the scar is the lasting expression of a wound. As the wound heals, it is bound to that expression.

There are fewer words than there are cells in the human organism. And yet, despite that, in the congregation of Polish words there are so many, many more than those we speak, write, or merely know. Permit me to attempt an elucidation of that statement with a metaphor. You, dear Sir, juggle something like four thousand words, and yet for each of these there is something like a hundred more that are not in reach of your milling arms. This does not mean that they do not exist, that they were never stored up in the grand magazine of speech. Now, in the present hour of history, the appreciation of the word is changing drastically. Jacek Dukaj is of the opinion that we live in the era of post-writing, and if such is the case, then it is an era of post-thinking too, marked by emotion and hysterics, panic and expressions that fall out of definite form, and instincts and manias chafed by the power of technology and its machinery, available to the masses.

For these several reasons, the word and its expression are deserving of our attention and, on account of their age, of respect. And humility, due to the fact that the word is pregnant in metaphorical and symbolical possibilities, which our ancient countrymen fathered upon them, outfitting them by their own inventiveness in additional meanings, just as a chamber inherited from grandmother or grandfather is refitted, transformed, or merely bettered through the introduction of new gadgets, or has its purpose entirely transformed. So many things, so many issues bind the living to the dead — too many to reckon! Each and every specialist of whatever fragment of today's hyperatomised man might come up with a long list of identities and analogies in this matter. However, the living and the dead are certainly linked by clouds, mists, storms, the sun, the rain, which in a mortal moment, each human being encloses in his eye; the sudden view of one's blood or the blood of others, which from the very first dawn of existence has flowed through each of our organisms, this binds them together, always red, that blood, flowing like the Styx, flowing and spurting out like wellsprings . . . And indeed, each and every word had its own premiere; its anonymous creator. Through each and every word there have flowed currents of pain and grumbling, calmness and tears, happiness and suffering, delight and curses, penetrating screams and focussed, meditative silence, rebellion, catastrophe, defeat. Through each and every one of them has flitted or flits or shall flit the creative vein. According to the maximalist-alchemists, the word is a blood vessel, seething with the blood that rushes through it. The art of literature, and poetry especially, is that which amongst all others remains the most 'national', meaning that it arises from the language of fathers and mothers, communities in little father- and motherlands, no matter whether matriarchies or patriarchies, and it is an indifferent matter how brilliantly it may be translated into another linguistic idiom — even so it always loses something of its cells, bits, pieces, orts, and ingredients, its whole incantatory foundation.

The poet charges the word with fascination, and the afflatus, which narrows the distance between him and the word, between subject and word-object, is reciprocal inebriation. The poet treats the word as a being, and in this sense, he becomes its chanticleer or, to set it more colourfully in Mazovian slang, its *piejak*, its 'screecher'. The poet stumbles about in the carpel of the word like a bee drunk on nectar. He, or she, is a highly qualified keeper of the word, reformer and navigator and renewer—in that phase, in which the word effects a transformation or a transposition from the status quo of the system biological and grammatical, political and poetical, social and metaphysical. Gottfried Benn, who was both a poet and a physician, which is important to note considering his viewpoints, once wrote, 'Human existence presupposes the existence of a nervous system; volatility, breeding, an immense awareness of facts, art. To suffer is to suffer consciously. The dead do not suffer. In a word, life means life awakened, awoke, aroused'. These opinions of Benn illuminate my intuitional realisation that the letter of the word is conjured by the nervous (sensitive) system of the poet. Later, it resonates in the receptor, chafing his own innervation. I beg your pardon for using such slogans as rooster, bee, carpels, pollens, and blooms, but nature, amidst which I live and work, provides a natural set of metaphors; in nature, as I see it, in its most hidden and concealed depths, are rooted (though not literally) all of the styles and forms of the liberal arts. A glimpse into these structures, their penetration, was and is the domain of artistic vision and only secondarily of microscopes and telescopes. But visions and laboratories often go hand in hand. In the case of the poet, this possesses an alchemical character, while for the physicist, a scientific and facultative one. The word is a great challenge—ho, ho dear Sir, so great a challenge! Each of these, especially the most powerful among them like God, Salvation, Hope, Love, Truth, Beauty, Justice, Good, Responsibility, Service, Loyalty, Friendship, Homeland, Earth. And at this juncture, where I break off my list, I might ask you, Sir, to continue it with, so to speak, your own. And so the word is a great challenge, and before we take it in hand, we ought to mature to the task. To ripen unto it. Meanwhile we use it, chew it like a cud, turning it this way and that as we please and when we please, bestowing upon it the most extreme expression—in the form of spittle or a shrug of the shoulders. But we are not the rulers of the word, we are not lords of the word; at most we are its vassals or slaves. We are born in strophes of words and it is through their agency that we sense, take note of, and think the world. The frontiers of our tongue are the frontiers of our cognition. We peer closely, we solicit, we rummage about, and still we are unable to make out the edges, the foundations, to say nothing of the vaults of the linguistic strophe of the tongue into which we were cast at birth. And because we can neither mature nor ripen to the word, we prefer to mutilate it like little girls who tear the arms and legs from their dolls or like little boys for whom the greatest thrill at playtime is some catastrophe, some cataclysm undergone by their toys. In the vulgar imagination, the word is something less than the life of man, and so you can tread it flat like a frog, poison it like a fox, or hack it up, hash it like a slab of meat. But such thinking is from the get-go mistaken, just as the mass of human judgements and adjudications is mistaken. The only certainty is the mist, and another—that we stumble about lost in that mist. And the word? It is the word that leads us to the threshold of the eternal landscape and sketches, despite its limitations, the horizon of the limitless. It possesses within it the hidden appeal of tracking that which is eternal and incomprehensible. Attacking being, doing violence to its ontological forms, we simultaneously degrade and humiliate the word that described, penetrated, and elevated it, being as it is an incursion of spirit and light, the intrusion of a solemn magical element into our midst. And so it is not for the word to mature to you and your perspective; no, you ought to ripen to the word along with everything that it invokes. Whether you like it or not, each and every poet possesses a hidden particle of faith in the victory of the word over death, in its elevation of life as Christ elevated His body to resurrection. Without this maximalist programme, without faith, everything associated with the *lingua* remains a mere game, a charade, a puzzle for minds weary and bored with the content and nourishment of life. And furthermore, the word asks nothing of you, demands nothing—in contrast to other people and your environment, beginning with your parents and relatives and ending with your boss, your lover, your friends, and the massive entertainment industry, and the consumer, political, and military complexes. The most the word searches for is *the perfect host*—the poet or the mystic. Legions of us take no note of what I'm writing about to you,

Sir, no note at all—quite simply, the issue is not to be found in their lives. Please don't take that as blame or criticism. I simply feel that they have other things to do and that's fine, as long as they do them with love. Yet all human tasks are only brilliant thanks to words, sparkling like all the waters of the world, of which both their tiny ripples and immense tidal waves glitter in the light. What is it that we will regret on our deathbed? Will it not be that we did not mature to life, that somehow we missed it in its passing? Where was it—we shall ask—that life? Life slid past us, its promises evaporated, and now we have to die. More than once do I wonder to what extent this regret is bound up with the word and the task it presents to each of us. To what extent does this regret emerge from the lack of contact between the word and our flesh, against which it merely grazed without incarnation, without entering into any even momentary intercourse therewith? Because the word incarnate is the word to which one has matured, with which the flesh has scarred over, crossing the threshold of its action, unfurling like a flag all its hidden senses, its senses eclipsed. Jorge Luis Borges once said, 'I regret never having been capable of happiness'. On his deathbed, Aldous Huxley is reputed to have said, 'The one thing I regret is that I could have been more pleasant to people'.

And so writers of the calibre of this Argentinian and that Briton, who were both intimately associated with the word, for whom it was an instrument of their labour, even they admitted to not having risen to the task that the word sets before man. And so they departed from the world in disappointment at being incapable of happiness and tenderness.

I am certain, dear Sir, that you are not unfamiliar with the ancient Indian ritual of becoming blood brothers by a reciprocal slicing of the wrists and a compression of both wounds together. Such was the custom of the Indians. As for the Saami, having hunted down a reindeer, they would bleed it and drink that blood so as to unite with the spirit of the animal, allowing it, in a sense, to continue to live in them. It's much the same thing, only that the Indian became one with a living person, while the Saam with a dead animal. In the Book of Kings, Moses wrote that the soul has its seat in the blood. Blood is the most noble substance in the world, and whenever man wished to say something great to God, something ineffable, he always made a blood sacrifice to Him. Ineffable? These rituals expressed the striving of the human being to a scarring together with God, another man, and a beast, and were always accompanied by words whispered, declaimed, and chanted in a solemn manner, words of the greatest weight pulsing out like blood from an open vein.

But please, dear Sir, never go so far! I beg you to be reasonable and to receive these meditations of mine in a symbolic dimension and to think them over in said dimension, thereupon to incarnate them in life. To fulfil such a task is indeed a difficult matter, and so it shall remain. Unless we're only doing it for show (in the media) or completing an examination to prove our mastery of the subject. But then we've tainted it with the bacillus of the slapdash. For the secret of the task is not to master it by rote or perform it for show, but to come to know it and to incarnate it as words in the praxis of living, endowing in this manner our existence with sense, here and now, bestowing upon it a solemn dimension and this particular mark, by which we come to know that life is the greatest privilege with which we meet day by day, and our constant griping and the demands we make of life, our bitching and moaning, always come to a bad end, because fate doesn't much cotton to being pressured or irritated.

One more thing. I beg you to stop writing me with complaints of how bored you are, Sir. Boredom is a powerful and extensive phenomenon that encumbers the shoulders of strong characters and creative titans alone. There are so many good and noble deeds we can perform in the face of being and on behalf of being. Please Sir, have a glance around the area in which you find yourself and discover, for yourself, how many things there are that are crying out for sympathy, for elevation, for amelioration. One good word, one good deed, every day—even this turns out to be too burdensome a task for people. But in order for you to glimpse the truth of anything, Sir, you must fulfil at least one elementary condition: forget, Sir, about that paper cut on your finger, or at least try and scar it over with someone or something.

THREE BACKGROUNDS

Our beginnings are difficult to make out, at least as difficult as is our end. How can we know, for example, what our last words will be? And there's absolutely no way of remembering the first word of our poem of initiation, even the one that dubbed us a poet. The imaginations of most people prefer to dwell on those last words expressed by famous men, writers, philosophers, artists, right before death. According to Mark and Matthew, Christ on the Cross said 'My God, my God, why hast Thou abandoned me?' while, according to John, 'It is finished', and according to Luke: 'Father, into Thy hands, I commend my spirit'. Supposedly, Beethoven said 'Applaud! The comedy is over'. Goethe: 'More light!' The last sentence written by Frida Kahlo in her journal reads 'I hope that death is joyful. I hope I never come back here'. When one of his numerous disciples asked him for a final message, Karl Marx chased them all away with the strong words: 'Get out of here! Last words are for dolts who didn't say enough during life'. Beginnings, on the other hand, are scattered. They head in many directions, pressed upon by so many futures—who ever dug up the first words of poetry, poetic lines, strophes, rhymes, images? An end is concentrated, focussed in a one-directional way on dying, which nears in constantly crashing waves—for that reason it's easier to lurk upon the approach of spoken or written word as epilogue.

And yet I shake my memory like an apple tree in hopes that its fruit will still be juicy, filling, beautifully round. Of course, this is all an illusion, however beautiful an illusion it may be. It's easier for me to recall the first poems, the first readings, and above all the first words, magical words, even if incomprehensible, like the words of a ritual, bitter words experienced by the senses as if they were tangible things. The poet is the fascinator of the word, which appears to him as a being. Despite that, poetry is intangible. When you awaken, these ungraspable things vanish, but when they appear, it is like a sudden glow or blow, as Tsvetaeva puts it. It is the incarnation of the 'metaph' in the physical, corporal, tangible world. The earthquakes occasioned by that intrusion of poetry into life are of a psychophysical character, and the fissures they make in a person are enduring; in one's tongue they become permanent scars.

What image is the first to fall when I shake the apple tree of memory? Delight, in grade school, with the beauty of my classmate Żaneta G. This delight knocked me completely out of the heretofore well-worn grooves of my boyhood, and the object of that delight was like a lighthouse, the pulsing beam of which attracted my emotions, my thoughts, and my dreams. Because I was a rather shy lad, I would slip little scraps of paper with poems I'd written into the pockets of her coat as if this would pry open my lips in regard to her. This coat, of a biscuit colour, hung in the cloak-room, and inside its hood was a beret; in the pockets were woollen mittens, both attached by a long thread of wool passed through the sleeves so as to prevent either of the gloves from getting lost. The poet expresses the continual wonder of existence and asks, how did it come about that existence exists? That there is this, that there is that? The polar opposites of this expression are delight and terror, love and despair, and so a state that is stretched between hymn and elegy. My delight with Żaneta G. and my despair arising from the terror that such a great beauty was out of my reach, this was my first experience of the duality of existence, as well as a symbol of the poetry that my state required. This delight simultaneously exemplified an as-yet unrealised, and yet already experienced, tongue, which rushes off to the battlefield when challenged by something concrete, a detail, something unique emerging from the background. And thus my eye, bored to tears by the background of the everyday trudge to school, and the tired old classroom, and the tired old lessons, and the masses of all the other pupils, fished out for itself a concrete incarnation — these very eyes and no other, this very manner of smiling, of tilting the head — in a word, the eye came to rest upon that other loneliness and love, as Rilke wrote: in a 'vigil over someone's loneliness'. It's impossible to love everything, a background, an abstraction, a concept, or a generality, and above all, large numbers. The concrete that is fished out of the background is a sign of tenderness and love, and like every phenomenon, object, animal, the individual person is by nature metaphysical, even though many of them are burdened by an inborn dullness. The concrete strengthens the memory; the background weakens it.

Let us pass on to my experience with letters. Take the invocation of Adam Mickiewicz with which he begins *Pan Tadeusz*, that most important metaphysical epic in Polish poetry. The modulation, the incantation of those words so charmed me that I determined to describe my native Sopot in just such lines — the city through which I walked to school, its overgrown gardens with its mute statues, its non-functioning fountains, mysterious apartment blocks and the scent wafting from their stairwells, which was a mixture of musty basements and the apples stored in them, good perfume and colonial goods. I was quite pleased with the linguistic effects of these little verses, and because I knew no other poets, in my mind I declared myself to be the one and only poet on earth. And so there was me and that 'stray' from Lithuania, who had after all been dead for some time by then. And this was my sin of pride, which in the hierarchy of poetic sins is the most dangerous of all, as any talent that one possesses is no merit of one's own. One's work, yes of course, but then one's words, rhythm, and orchestration, all of these are suggested to one, bestowed upon one from without. In the case of my inspiration by Mickiewicz's words, I myself emerged from a background.

And there is one more concrete, as palpable as any apple shaken from the tree of memory. Over the years, I have visited many Polish monuments in the provinces: cloisters and monasteries, estates, palaces, and castles. Under the influence of Grochowiak's poem 'The Custodian', I wrote some strophes, each of which began with an anaphora, 'I'd like to become a custodian'. I no longer have that poem — it vanished like so many others scribbled down in the graphomanic fervour of my early youth. But the inditing of this little work was inspired not only by Grochowiak's long poem but also by the interiors of those castles, palaces, and cloisters, both those that had been opened to visitors and those that still only had such potential. And anyway, the attraction I had to such objects remains with me to this day—this attraction to buildings, parks, and gardens. Only after the passage of many, many years did I come to realise that by hacking out that little path, I was blazing my future destiny. Since 1997, I have been the custodian of museums dedicated to two poets here in Mazovia: Gałczyński and Kajka. Now, the word 'custodian' doesn't have the best associations for me, because in Polish *kustosz* reminds one of *kurz* [dust] and *kostucha* [Grim Reaper], for which reason I define the profession humorously: as this custodian wiping the dust from display cases and artefacts. And in this manner, we arrive at a third background. And so, led on by Grochowiak's poem, I arrived at the threshold of the future, from the background of which I chiselled out my present occupation and role of custodian, a literary custodian, who, in service to the memory of other poets, cares for his own little plot of letters as well.

WOJCIECH KASS was born in 1964 in Gdynia. He is poet, essayist, and diarist. In 1989, he graduated with a degree in Polish Literature from the University of Gdańsk, defending his master's thesis under the direction of Professor Maria Janion. Since 1987, he has brought out nearly twenty volumes of poetry and has been nominated for important awards several times; In 2019, his *Objawy* [Revelations] was awarded the Fr Jan Twardowski Prize for Poetry. He has written on the poets Czesław Miłosz and Konstanty Ildefons Gałczyński; since 1997, he has worked and lived at the museum of the latter poet in Pranie, Mazovia. He is a member of the Association of Polish Writers (SPP), the Polish PEN Club, and ZAiKS. He has been awarded the Bronze Cross of Merit (2006) and the bronze and silver Gloria Artis medals (2015) by the Republic of Poland. His poems have been translated into many languages.

Charles S. Kraszewski

I'M NOT ASKING FOR MUCH

O that some dog would take me for a walk.
O that some dog, a Rottweiler were best
or Giant Schnauzer, or eventually a Čuvač
would get off his ass and adopt me and take me
for a walk in Hyde Park.
I promise to behave myself.
I promise not to make Master or Mistress blush.
Although I am of that humble perhaps even base
species Homo quasi sapiens
I know how to be a good boy.
I will not chase the birds along the Serpentine
like the spoilt child
of too lenient a mother
Colin I'm going to count to forty-five...
I promise not to lunge at the runners suddenly
where the path narrows
near Queen Caroline's monument.
and if He/She lets me tumble about with other people
on the lawn near Physical Energy
all of my nips will be play bites, pretend.
I shall not attempt—I swear—to mount
any bitch who happens to cross my path.
I know how to be a good boy. If my Master
or Mistress pauses our trot at the Lido Café
I will lay me down calmly at her feet.
I will not beg annoyingly or try
to steal a treat from the table
completely satisfied to lap any sort of tea
they pour into my bowl
panting nirvanically and winking
from time to time
in the direction of the other
well-behaved people.

Charles S. Kraszewski   283

CODICES OF THE CONQUERED

Without all that much fuss, in point of fact
we Aztecs consented to all that:
the change of bosses in Tenochtitlan,
mass baptisms in the clogged canals
and even the supersession of Nahautl
by Castellano.

First of all, no one in his right mind
ever believed, really,
that that debauched crybaby Montezuma
was the son of god.
Our gods were imperfect
but come on.

Second (à propos)
only the thickest of the thickheaded believed
that the sun was thirsty for the blood of innocents
and, if it were not offered him, he'd turn away
his shining face, never to rise again.
Beyond that the stench of rotting flesh
at the foot of the temple stairs
had become, to put it gently,
noisome.
And that God the Spaniards brought us in exchange?
Hey, it's us who eat *Him*
and under quite palatable accidentia.

But as for our language, well, too bad, really.
Cemenahuatl's prettier than *mundo* don't you think?
Coatepantli says so much more than *friso*.
But what's to be done.
A peso's a peso.

And it was the peso that overcame our armies
putting an end to the flower wars.
No great loss that, indeed, but
they did make of us a nation of shopkeepers
and pimps.
Everything's for sale

and you won't coax coin from Spanish pockets
with homely syllables like
Quen tlazohti
Oquichtli ixtlahuaz nochi...

But what's true is true:
our great writers do live on
in their more colourful logographic strips
torn from the living flesh of
the Codex Ixtlilxhchitl
the Codex Borbonicus
the Codex Borgia and so forth
framed under glass and tastefully displayed
above the bathroom sinks
of the chic wives of officials
on the middle rung of their career.

THE NAMING OF THE BEASTS

Next, Adam said 'Canis familiaris. This one will be my friend'.
And then a lion trotted up along with a lamb.
'Panthera leo', and (after a little pause)
'ovis aries. But we'll call that little darling agnus'
(and the Lord God smiled).
There was also a rattlesnake 'Crotalus cerastes'
which a brown eagle ('aquila chrysaetos')
placed gently at the feet of Adam, until
having received their names, they flew back off
like the best of friends . . .
It would take too long to mention all the animals
here and now, amidst this sinful world:
Ursus maritimus . . . Salmo trutta . . . Lycosa singoriensis . . .
but this took place — let's not forget — in Paradise
where there was neither labour nor exhaustion.
'And you?' the Lord asked Adam in the end. 'Who will you be?'
'Me?' he replied. 'I want to be Gauleiter'.
'Idiot!' Eve hissed, 'Be more ambitious!'
with a quick sharp elbow to the ribs.

YAWN

I saw the best minds of my generation, and they were
nothing much to look at
compared to that generation past, or so I thought
until I came to realise that anyone can do automatic
writing in semen,
that grammar is important, and that a halting school-
boy familiarity with Dostoevsky is not just pretentious, it's
embarrassing;
that there are some good aspects to censorship and that
just because a book is banned, that doesn't make it worth
reading;
that not everything can or should be blamed on drugs,
and that if they didn't contract syphilis from all those curi-
ous triangles ménages-à-septs and casual knee-tremblers in
men's room stalls, then they have no excuse whatsoever;
I saw the best minds of my generation dressed in shirts
from the waist up
and in trousers or skirts from the waist down according
to their ever more arbitrary gender or peculiar inclination;
Like all the best minds of all past generations they walked
on two feet wearing their right shoes on their right feet,
their left on their left;
When the best stomachs of my generation began to grum-
ble those rationally shod feet carried them into kitchens
stocked with vegetables chicken broth frutti di mare or the
frozen body parts of mammals among which they picked
out something to eat according to taste philosophy or other
peculiar determining factor;
And thus the sugar-level spiked in the best and worst
blood of my generation as it had done in those of the past,
otherwise there would be no more haphazard procreation
of generations best worst or indifferently middling;
I heard the best lips of my generation exclaim *Ah me
there is nothing new under the sun*;
Perhaps after all those lips as good as they were did not
belong to the best minds of my generation,
for they did nothing but repeat a lament stretching back

at least to the best mind of that generation which came to be around tenth century B C;

although modern scholarship has discovered that the chap in question stole that sentiment from another chap representing the best minds of generations Mesopotamian after which he

strove to shred burn or crush according to the type of material it was writ upon all copies of the earlier chap's work baked on clay brushed on papyrus or incised in granite or obsidian;

Such a great mind that, of his and subsequent generations who first realised that he who controls the presses controls the oppressed see our earlier sentiments concerning censorship;

Then sick to death in Brindisi Virgil returning from his piratical journeys round Odysseus' Greece was next to realise this *Burn my epic* he said *Stop your snivelling Horace and burn my shit if you're not inclined to burn Homer instead, which, to be perfectly honest, would be preferable though slightly impractical* —

a lesson not yet learnt by the best minds of my generation who, intent on making a précis of the scriptures boiled them all down to one short pithy statement *What is truth?*

A significant achievement reducing 900,000+ words to three;

But tell me what's stopping us from getting rid of them too and starting over? Well, this is the truth, *What I have written I have written* from the lips of the same dude who said *What is truth* as if to say *Here you are this is truth leave it alone no matter how much it hurts*;

In the beginning, like it or not, was the Word.

NATURE INÉPUISABLE

In the evening
high up on the cathedral façade
in front of everybody
a male pigeon takes himself to
a female of his kind
between the very slippers of St Syagrius.

Naturally, St Syagrius is scandalised.
So many people on the Place Rossetti
aroused enough with wine as it is
undressed enough as it is,
but hardly had he raised his arm to scold them
than he froze
petrified.

AT THE CORNER OF ALETHEIA AND THARSESIS

καί νύκ' ὀδυρομένοισι φάνη ῥοδοδάκτυλος Ἠώς,
εἰ μὴ ἄρ' ἄλλ' ἐνόησε θεὰ γλαυκῶπις Ἀθήνη...

You ask me why the gods will not restrain
the horses of the dawn as once they did
at Penelope's behest, though this is Athens
and this bed too is made of olive wood.
Well first of all because they're shameless braggarts
who promise more than they're able to deliver,
meanwhile Our Lord has more important things
to do. But even if they did exist
those little godlets, they would know quite well
that I'm not going anywhere
with flail-shaped oar slung over my shoulder;
that I will never ever,
ever
leave You.

ON THE LAWN AT VRCHLICKÉHO SADY

On the lawn at Vrchlického Sady
across from the Main Station
and the cheapest bedding in Prague
stands a red-haired girl, barefoot, dirty
with scabs on her calves
playing Pergolesi
on a violin.

This is not a poem about how
art can surprise you when you least expect it.
This is not a poem about how
everybody has his or her own story
everybody deserves our respect
everybody has his hidden depths.

This is a poem about a girl
with dirty feet
and scabby calves
playing Pergolesi on a violin.

Charles S. Kraszewski   291

AT BONAPARTE

a little man
enters the bus.

There is no place free.
So he pushes himself politely
—*pardon pardon*—
through the standing crowd
and grabs a rail
at the last moment
before the bus lurches forward.

Oh la vache!

The momentum tosses him
onto the knees of a young woman
knocking the phone
out of her hand.

pardon, mademoiselle!
pas de problème pas d'souci

And so he girds himself in courage
and asks
how one might get to Sainte-Hélène?

The little man
in the Superdry t-shirt
and New York Yankees cap
on his head
(in all the wrong colours)
must get out at Parc Phoenix
and take the nr. 2 tram
towards Port Lympia
in order to get to Sainte-Hélène.

Merci merci
says the timid little man
who won't dare
occupy any empty place
even should one become available.

WHERE ARE YOU NOW, ALBERT-ERNEST CARRIER-BELLEUSE?

Death walks along the Promenade du Paillon
and suddenly the retired women sitting
beneath the limp bronze dick of David
begin to sketch with their left hands.
Astonished, they stare at their left hands.
And Death chuckles. It's her little joke.

Death walks along the Promenade du Paillon.
Suddenly, a sexy young girl in a white blouse,
a short skirt, with legs to die for in red high heels
shivers, hearing a whisper at her fragrant ear:
Seven years, six months, twelve days.
Or maybe it was just a cool breeze
from the water jets? *Hee hee hee* Death laughs.

Squealing and laughing the children enter and exit
the wooden skeleton of the whale.
Haa! Haa! Haa! screeches Death in the form of a gull
stamping its webbed feet on the bronze coiffeur
of Masséna, who smiles painfully
as he knows full well
that there is no exit from the skeleton.

Charles S. Kraszewski   293

TAKE THAT, MR NIETZSCHE

I bring you glad tidings
revealed unto me in the subway
beneath the Náměstí Jiřího z Poděbrad:
the end of the era of the death of God.
For in the kiosk hangs a calendar:
I am a Goddess. Glory in the depths
to the goddess. Or goddesses. For after all
we're still unable to state with certainty
if there's one goddess or
twelve goddesses and anyway
the theologians have not yet proved capable
of defining the extent of her/their
power, nor have they come to a solution of the problem
is her/their power to last *in saecula saeculorum*
or is it to peter out at each month's end?

AFTER A LONG ROAD LEADING NOWHERE

The tajchy *(Slovak regionalism from the German 'Teich')*
are manmade freshwater terraced pools constructed in the
early eighteenth century, when Banská Štiavnica led Europe
in the mining of gold and silver. Their pristine waters are
full of life, and popular with swimmers, despite the chill
(the town lies in the Tatra foothills), and with sunbathers
too (nudists mainly keep to the far side of the tajch, away
from the path leading up Glanzenberg).
> —Stefan Tejk's Atlas of Hierophanies

Those fish in the emerald water of the *tajch*
are not the same fish
as back in November.
They look the same, but they're not.
I'd be interested to learn
what they're thinking
those fish in the *tajch* in August.
I see them and I ask myself
are they trout
or *blatniaky*
or *jalce.*
They see me and they think
that I'm the same shadow
they saw last week
which means in fish years
two Novembers ago.

No, it's not like that.
They swim near my shadow and think
glubb glubb
which in the tongue of fish means
bread bread.

And the tall trees that ring the *tajch*
sink their roots deep into the moist soil,
stretching their branches high towards the sun
lazily, deliciously
like beautiful young girls
getting up

Charles S. Kraszewski

from an afternoon nap.

And the trees think even less
than beautiful young girls.

And the water thinks even less than the trees.

CORSO UMBERTO

Every morning at 8:15
they pack themselves into the red sardine
can number 122
with their rafts
plastic soccer balls
beach umbrellas
folding boards with cheap sunglasses
and their own black bodies
to doze all the way to Fontane Bianche.

There, they'll wander up and down the beach
with inflatable ducks around their waists
with four straw hats perched on their heads
under the careful eye of the fellow
who holds their passports hostage.
If they have passports in the first place.

And the white folk stretched out on the sand
take no more notice of them
than the birds that skim above them in the blue.
Such is the measure of their contempt, their fear.

Yes yes
this is no *camp des saints.*
The bathers fear nothing but
cancer
aging
pregnancy
and any sort of death
save euthanasia.

Charles S. Kraszewski

MESJIDS OF MADISON AVE.

PleaseGodPleaseGodPleaseGodPleaseGod
    —Five year-old 'beauty pageant' contestant, awaiting
        the creepy judges' determination of the winner
        of the grand prize in the 'Supremes Division'.

PleaseGodPleaseGodPleaseGodPleaseGod
    —The dam that dropped the above-mentioned whelp,
                                    five years before.

Oh, mesjids of Madison Avenue,
innermost of inner sanctums
undescried by the worshipper's eye from the sidewalk,
undefiled by the soles of the Nike Air Max Conquer Boot
you have commanded him to purchase
from the particoloured minaret outside Madison Square
    Garden;
far above the overflowing crowds each toting flashy credos
of responsibly recycled polymers and paper
(Macy's, NBA Store, Juicy Couture)
more sincere than the smudgy crosses
on Ash Wednesday foreheads
(who has time for that, after all, when there's a sale on
at Lord and Taylor?)
nor are you confined to a Vatican ghetto
between Fifth and Park Avenues;
discreetly diffused like the Church of Ogilvy and Mather
throughout the whole globe (in Riyadh too —
who says only one faith in the Arabian Peninsula?)
your scripture, your Biblia Pauperum Divitumque
surrounds us with the good news
Buy It Buy It You Deserve It
from bus stop poster to ad-carriers on taxis
to the scrolling LEDs of Times Square and Piccadilly Circus
to the billboards above the crowded helix
that circles down into the Lincoln Tunnel,
that bears us down into the gullet of the Lincoln Tunnel
like passengers on Geryon's back;

the voices of your muezzins
call to us from television and movie screen
over the radio and subliminally, from beneath
the muzak in The World's Biggest Store
There's Something Here For Everyone;
O omnipresent, O potentially omniscient
Based on Your Preferences May We Suggest For You
O almost omnipotent, for
if ever I forget thee . . .
Well, if ever I forget thee, thy multitudinous tongues
will be silenced forever,
cleft to the roof of thy palate;
how easy it would be to kill this god —
Turn away, turn away Dick Whittington . . .
BUT
What else do we have here?
It's Your Money, Use it When You Need It
what little this big world has to offer us
you promise us —
how easy it is to believe your pitch,
Just Save the Requisite Number of Boxtops
Or Agree to Participate in At Least Three Offers
From Our Sponsors Offer Not Good in Alaska
Hawaii Puerto Rico or anywhere else
one can find a semi-autonomous realm
of self-respect and intellectual maturity;
Then Your Free I-Pad Will Be On Its Way To You.
It's as simple as that;
Become A Wheel Watcher, then make sure
to pray fifty times daily in the direction
of your digital mihrab so as not to miss
the twenty-four hour window of grace,
the day of jubilee,
But Call In And Win Your All-Expense Paid
Trip to Sandals Resort or Some Other Tropical
Ante-chamber of Hell,
With Golf-Course and Hot Stone Massage Therapy
Sushi Bar and For A Small Additional Cost
Give the Wheel One Final Spin
You Can't Win if You Don't Play

Charles S. Kraszewski

O, my heart is restless until it rests in . . .
Well, my heart is restless.
But there are pharmaceuticals for that
And I deserve to Live Free of Fear
You know just what I need, Astra Zeneca
You know me better than I know myself,
and out of the bowels of your compassion
will even finance my habit, if needed;
Foolish the man who saith in his heart there is no Astra Zeneca
Let him take the simple ten-question online quiz
to see whether or not he's clinically depressed
even though He's Going to Disneyland.
You Can't Take it With You?
Don't cry for him, Bargaintina,
he got just what he deserved
according to the research results
for his particular demographic;
he shopped, until he dropped
into the latest model casket;
a happy death, the good sick beast,
exiting through the gift shop.

HERE IS NO GOD BUT MAMMON AND DAMNÉD IS HIS PROFIT

There was a fire in the church last night, and no,
not the dim cherry glow
of the tabernacle lamp
burning like a silent torch outside the great man's tent
at the Milvian camp:
Hic ego sum, Imperator,
In hoc signo vinces;
no, a flame voracious, like that three years before
that sucked the cotton swabs to sooty pinches,
the swabs that scrubbed the oil from the altar stone
after the sacristy bell-rope (so long forgot)
was garrotted into a knot;
after the tiny golden doors
of the altar of repose
were set ajar
upon the evacuation of the Host,
the crating of ciboria and all the sacred store
of monstrance, thurible and navicula;
when, desacralised, the building stood alone,
abandoned, empty for the first time
since it was consecrated in 1899.

The harsh moon shone down through the clear plastic panes
where once brooded the gem-clad saints
of Hungary and Slovakia, all sold
now to a new parish in Maryland; so cold
a dry white light never seized the pews
(right side with brim-clips for the men's hats,
on the left side of the aisle, the widows sat),
garishly spotlighting each Golgothan bruise
on the Saviour's body, nailed to the tree
painted on the apse (by Grace Bros. and Company),
His right side ripped by Longinus' lance,
His battered knee-caps
(for He fell thrice in that cruel Totentanz
we reenacted each Friday in Lent).
And now our temple curtain, too, is rent.

Charles S. Kraszewski   301

No, the fire in the church last night
made (my apologies for the trite
but fitting cliché) a lurid light,
not warm and golden, like the lamps that burned
on Holy Thursday night, as we slowly turned
in procession near the communion rail, around the outer naves
behind Fr Janeka, who with humeral-veiled hands
bore Christ in the splendid monstrance, everyone genu-
    flecting in waves:
a woollen, wooden, plush and human sea
roaring those billowing, heart-drowning chants

Tantum ergo Sacramentum
Veneremur cernui;
Et antiquum documentum
Novo cedat Ritui;
Praestet fides supplementum
Sensuum defectui,

everyone, the old Slovak babas in kerchiefs,
the spare, whiskered vets who swore
allegiance to no flag, but a Person, back in the first war:
Franz Josef, then dear Blessed Karl the First;
the sodality girls in their short white skirts,
and Mom and Dad and the chief of police;
that honey-thick light reflecting molasses off pew-back
all the saints in the windows black
(light, all the light inside)
and the statues draped in purple, for Christ died
and Christ, the hidden God, would not arise
until the reborn sun should flood the Sunday skies
and send the rubies emeralds and topaz spilling
through Michael the Archangel and the villain
pinned sickly violet beneath his feet;

no, the fire in the church last night was set
by someone who broke in,
said Hakim,
who owns the rectory, church hall and shell
that housed the font where the residue of Hell
was once washed from my infant skin

and I was given a fighting chance;
'I bin tryin', he said
'Shit, man, I had planz
Fo' dat place; I wanna do sumpin' good
Fo' all da kidz in da naybahood'.
(Now, all the old Slovaks wonder if it was him).
'But dat ain't true;
I do
Have a itty-bitty rap-sheet but dat's in de past;
I'm straight's an arrow now, man, has you ast
Dem people livin 'roun 'heah?
Cuz dey don' like me none, man.
Butchoo tell me: how can
I fix dis shit up now?
I got no insurance.
How?
An' I wuz gonna open up a nice gym
Fo' all da kidz in de naybahood'.
Thus Hakim,
Proprietor of what used to be
The Roman Catholic Parish of St Anthony.

When my cousin Nick broke down the narthex door
and lugged the swelling fire hose across the dirty tiled floor
of the cold vestibule,
he caught his boot against a metal stool
and fell across the ropes
of a regulation size boxing ring.
Who woulda guessed that was there?
And thus end three cruel years
of appeals to three bishops and two popes —
in sum, ten deaf ears.
For the diocese was in arrears
(and all the restive faithful know, damn it, just why).
And still, pinned up on high,
Christ, on His Cross, with sooty stockinged feet
Stares through dirty plexiglass across a broken street.

*Coda: Le 25 juin 2024, à la porte de l'église Saint-Augustin et
    Saint-Martin à Nice, un infirme m'a offert une carte postale
    à l'effigie de Saint Antoine de Padoue. Peut-être par hazard.*

I was eight years old when I wrote my first composition approximating verse. It was a ballad about the Vietnam War set to a plastic toy guitar, out of tune, strummed on open strings. *Ahem.* What does an eight-year-old in 1970 know about war? What does an eight-year-old know about anything?

In my case, a cynic might say, What's changed, fifty-four years on?

Be that as it may. We'll return to the guitar in a moment.

The first time I read a poet who moved me, that poet was Thomas Hardy. Ezra Pound got the chronology wrong when in *Guide to Kulchur* he praised Hardy, admitting to a 'vain regret that one couldn't have written novels for thirty years or whatever before courting the muses'. Because Hardy always wrote verse; he only turned to it exclusively after swearing off novel writing, following the 'Jude the Obscene' tempest in a teapot. But he's right in the main: nobody tells a story like Hardy, cleanly, leanly, with a compositional logic that suggests to the reader that what he says really couldn't be said in any other way; with a compositional ease that seems to flow as effortlessly as a score by Mozart. Or, in Pound's immortal words, 'poem after poem of Hardy's leaves one with nowt more to say'.

Hardy was also fond of form. Someone once said that 'Hardy never uses the same metre twice'. That's not correct (vide his numerous sonnets), but it almost is. He took an obvious delight in a variation of feet, line lengths, metrical turns on a dime ... For one example, I would have the reader glance at 'The Convergence of the Twain', the poem he wrote on the sinking of the Titanic. The first line of each of the short stanzas is iambic, sprightly, full of the confidence of the people who dubbed her unsinkable; then, each of these lines is immediately, and consistently, followed by a succession of jerky trochees, amphibrachs, and spondees, which interrupt the progress of the poem, retarding the flow and mimicking the slow sinking of the ship to the bottom of the Atlantic. I wish I could have written something like that. (We'll return to that thought, too, in a moment).

Hardy was an agnostic; I am not. Hardy was a pessimist, and more often than I would like to be, so am I. Hardy was the child of simple people and grew up in a traditional society, as did I. The first time I read his poem 'The Oxen', I was knocked flat with a satori of recognition: this was something I too learnt at my grandmother's knee (long before there were any poems or plastic guitars in my life):

> Christmas Eve, and twelve of the clock.
>   'Now they are all on their knees',
> An elder said as we sat in a flock
>   By the embers in hearthside ease.
>
> We pictured the meek mild creatures where
>   They dwelt in their strawy pen,
> Nor did it occur to one of us there
>   To doubt they were kneeling then.
>
> So fair a fancy few would weave
>   In these years! Yet, I feel,
> If someone said on Christmas Eve,
>   'Come; see the oxen kneel,
>
> 'In the lonely barton by yonder coomb
>   Our childhood used to know',
> I should go with him in the gloom,
>   Hoping it might be so.

There is a great love of animals that I share with Hardy (something also taught me by my grandmother). And so I find a great dignity in 'Winter in Durnover Field', along with an unmatched mastery of form:

Scene. A wide stretch of fallow ground recently sown with wheat, and frozen to iron hardness. Three large birds walking about thereon, and wistfully eyeing the surface. Wind keen from north-east: sky a dull grey.
    (Triolet)

ROOK.—Throughout the field I find no grain;
  The cruel frost encrusts the cornland!

STARLING. —Aye: patient pecking now is vain
   Throughout the field, I find . . .

ROOK.   —No grain!

PIGEON. —Nor will be, comrade, till it rain,
   Or genial thawings loose the lorn land
   Throughout the field.

ROOK.   —I find no grain:
   The cruel frost encrusts the cornland!

Here we have not only a story, but an entire Greek trag-edy, encompassed in six lines, and the way that Hardy opens our eyes to the respect we owe other creatures—for other heartrending poems of this sort, see 'The Blinded Bird' and 'The Mongrel'—is unsurpassed even by his great latter-day disciple Robinson Jeffers.

So, for all of these reasons, in answer to the question I posed the poets collected in this anthology, in my own case, the answer is Thomas Hardy. You wouldn't be holding this book in your hands, dear Reader, if it were not for him. And so, if I've been wasting your time and your experience has been infuriating rather than delightful, blame it on Hardy.

Recently an editor asked me for a short biogram to accompany some things of mine she'd accepted for pub-lication. I began with something like 'Poet and translator from the Polish . . .' and stopped there. Poet. It's such a big word. With so much bardic baggage, or scum, if you prefer, that accumulates round the stone the longer it stands in a field. So I went back and wrote 'Poet (Jesus, who isn't?) and translator from the Polish . . .' because it seems that there are so many poets in the world (too many?), so many people writing something approaching verse, and yet 'poet' seems more like a title bestowed than a profession. If I were a plumber, I'd have no problem starting off my biogram with 'plumber', i.e., the trade I'd apprenticed in and mastered; as for 'poet', it seems to me that none of us have any right to call ourselves by that name. At least, that's how I feel, in my case: it's for others to judge. Nor is this a discovery of my own. Back in Kraków in 1984 or 1985, I was sitting having a drink with a fellow sent over to Poland by the British Council. We were talking about Gerard Manley Hopkins, when the fellow mentioned that he wrote poetry as well. He said it casually; it just emerged from the conversation naturally. Just as naturally, as a young person infatuated with all that was poetic, I gushed 'You write poetry . . . ?' And his response — a welcome bucket of cold water poured over too seething a brow — 'who doesn't?'

I have no problem referring to myself as a translator. Although not as practical or obvious a craft as plumbing, it's just as easily verifiable. A person can call him or herself a 'poet', and yet the scribbling he or she commits can be such rubbish that people who know what poetry is might be inclined to call the self-nobilitation into question. But the fact that the poems found in this anthology were first written in Polish and are now appearing in English, thanks to my translation of the same — please note that I avoid any sort of qualitative assessment here; that too is not for me to do — means that I am a translator.

But let's get back to the guitar.

My adventure with that instrument didn't end with the composition of that 'song' on Vietnam. Throughout high school, and in my early college years, I played in a band.* I was the bass player. And although I came to love the bass, at first I picked it up because there was no one amongst my friends who had a bass or wanted to be the bass player. So, all right, I'll do it. People who dream of being bass players as youngsters are, I reckon, few and far between. Most bass players, I imagine, are like me: frustrated or supernumerary guitarists who take up the instrument because 'somebody has to do it'. The same thing is true of translators of verse. I don't think there are many people, excited by reading as a young person, who say, 'That's for me! I want to learn Magyar so as to translate Ferenc Juhász!' No, translators of

---

* Were we any good? A quick anecdote. A year or so after the band broke up, I discovered the revelation that was The Smiths. I said to a girl I was dating at the time (very knowledgeable about music, she was) 'If I ever got the band back together, that's the sort of music we'd play!' Without skipping a beat, horrified, she replied, 'Don't you dare!'

verse want to be poets. They write their own verse, and then, if they have more than one language, they find themselves so struck with what someone else has written in another tongue that they know, that they become jealous in a healthy way (Remember: 'I wish I could have written that!') and this moves them to do the next best thing: to recreate that poem in a different language.

And so, I suppose I need to modify what I said above about wanting to be Thomas Hardy. Besides him, I want to be Eli Dymowski, Artur Grabowski, Wojciech Kass, Krzysztof Koehler, Andrzej Kotański, Jakub Pacześniak, Adriana Szymańska, Teresa Tomsia, Michał Zabłocki...

CHARLES S. KRASZEWSKI a citizen of both the Republic of Poland and the United States, was born in the latter country in 1962. He spends his happiest hours drowsing on a beach listening to The Rutles. Outside of that, he is a literary translator, mostly from Polish, Czech, and Slovak. He has published five books of original poetry, three in English and two in Polish, and that's probably enough. He's also published two satirical novels and a play *Ismene*. A member of the Polish Association of Writers (SPP), Kraków branch, and the Union of Polish Writers Abroad (ZPPnO), London, he has been awarded the Gloria Artis medal (third class) by the Ministry of Culture of the Republic of Poland, as well as the ZPPnO award for the propagation of Polish culture abroad, and the ZAiKS award for translation into a foreign language.